Christian Assembly

"Here is a book filled with treasures. Drawing upon thorough research, confessional integrity, biblical literacy, and astute perception of church and world, the authors invite us into a rich conversation. Their immensely important question for any who care about the church's witness is: How do we know that this is church, and what are the signs that this assembly is truly the body of Christ? Join the conversation! We will all be richer for it."

> —**Bishop Robert A. Rimbo**
> Southeast Michigan Synod
> Evangelical Lutheran Church in America

Christian Assembly

Marks of the Church
in a Pluralistic Age

Gordon W. Lathrop and
Timothy J. Wengert

*for Werner —
with deep respect
for your leadership
in the church*

Gordon Lathrop

Fortress Press
Minneapolis

CHRISTIAN ASSEMBLY
Marks of the Church in a Pluralistic Age

Cover art by Diana Ong © SuperStock, Inc. Used by permission.
Book design: Beth Wright
Photo on p. 38 courtesy Gordon W. Lathrop

ISBN 0-8006-3660-0

The paper used in this publication meets the minimum requirements of American National Standard for Information Sciences—Permanence of Paper for Printed Library Materials, ANSI Z329.48-1984.

Manufactured in the U.S.A.
08   07   06   05   04   1   2   3   4   5   6   7   8   9   10

Contents

Abbreviations

Ap	Apology of the Augsburg Confession
BC 2000	*The Book of Concord*. Ed. Robert Kolb and Timothy J. Wengert. Minneapolis: Fortress Press, 2000.
BSLK	*Die Bekenntnisschriften der evangelisch-lutherischen Kirche.* 12th printing. Göttingen: Vandenhoeck & Ruprecht, 1998.
CA	Augsburg Confession
CR	*Corpus Reformatorum: Philippi Melanthonis opera quae supersunt omnia,* ed. Karl Bretschneider and Heinrich Bindseil, 28 vols. (Halle: A. Schwetschke & Sons, 1834–1860)
ELCA	Evangelical Lutheran Church in America
Ep	Epitome of the Formula of Concord
LC	Large Catechism
LW	*Luther's Works,* American edition. 55 vols. Philadelphia: Fortress Press, and St. Louis: Concordia, 1955–86.
MBW	*Melanchthons Briefwechsel: Kritische und kommentierte Gesamtausgabe: Regesten,* ed. Heinz Scheible, 10+ vols. (Stuttgart Bad Cannstatt: Frommann-Holzboog, 1977–). (The numbers refer to the number of the letters [see also *T1/T2/T3* below].)
MSA	*Melanchthons Werke in Auswahl (Studienausgabe),* ed. Robert Stupperich, 7 vols. (Gütersloh: Gerd Mohn, 1951–1975).

PL	J. P. Migne, ed., *Patrologia Latina,* 217 vols. (Paris, 1844–55).
SA	Smalcald Articles
SC	Small Catechism
SD	Solid Declaration
T1/T2/T3	*Melanchthons Briefwechsel: Kritische und kommentierte Gesamtausgabe: Texte,* ed. Richard Wetzel, 3+ vols. (Stuttgart Bad Cannstatt: Frommann-Holzboog, 1991–). (See also *MBW* above.)
Tr	Treatise on the Power and Primacy of the Pope
WA	*Luthers Werke: Kritische Gesamtausgabe (Schriften).* 66+ vols. (Weimar: H. Böhlau, 1883–).
WA TR	*Luthers Werke: Kritische Gesamtausgabe: Tischreden.* 6 vols. (Weimar: H. Böhlau, 1912–21).

Preface

The book before you seeks to answer the questions, How do you know the Christian church when you encounter it? What are its marks?

The questions themselves—urgent for some people, theoretical for others, perhaps quaint or pitiful for others—are quite simple. But at the time of the Reformation, these questions became the grounds for such profound pastoral advice and such careful ecclesial organization that the Reformation proposals and confessions continue to have fresh import for the common life of Christians in our own day. Various lists were given: "Word and sacrament" was one. The seven characteristics listed by Luther in 1539 made up another. "Bath and table, prayer and word" was another. But together these lists meant to bear witness to an event: God acting in the midst of real assemblies to bring human beings to faith, clothe them in salvation, and make them together a community of witness to the triune mercy. Together these lists meant to bear witness to an idea of church utterly dependent on the confession that God justifies us by grace alone through faith. Taken seriously, the marks of the church can be revolutionary in their ecumenical significance, existentially powerful in their gracious offer to seekers, concretely helpful to pastors and congregational leaders, acutely important to theologians. As this book discusses the "marks of the church"—the way that the church can be known—it seeks to explore that continuing practical and theological import.

This book is thus an essay in Lutheran ecclesiology. But it ought not be seen as only for Lutherans. When Lutherans discuss the church, they hope to be making a proposal to all Christians. The matters that Lutherans call "the marks" are gifts that are given by God to every Christian community, regardless of "denomination." And discussion of their present meaning belongs to us all. This book, then—though it understands itself as the voices of only two current Lutheran teachers—dares to be such an ecumenical proposal.

For the questions that relate to the marks of the church do indeed belong to us all: How do we find a church we can trust? How do we rejoice in diversity and yet find ourselves united? What, if anything, remains "universal" in an age of pluralism and postmodernism? What things should be accented in church life? What things are less important? What is church for? Or, for that matter, what is preaching or sacrament or worship or ministry or mission for?

The questions can be put in another way. If church, at its basis, is a "participating local assembly," as both the New Testament and the current liturgical movement seem to say, and if we have lots of assemblies, small and large, virtual and real, in our pluralistic times, then how does one know when any given assembly is "church"? And how shall these assemblies encourage and admonish each other, rejoice with each other, sends signs of communion to each other, have a sense that they are one assembly in all the world?

In what follows, Timothy Wengert approaches these questions from the perspective of Reformation studies. He demonstrates that the idea of such "marks"—the very proposal of such an idea at all—comes uniquely from the polemical and pastoral work of Martin Luther and can be seen as the central ecclesial implication of the doctrine of justification. The idea was subsequently refined and developed by Philip Melanchthon. Wengert then pursues the pastoral and ecumenical importance of the idea in studies of the Lutheran confessional writings and of Luther's sermons. Chapters 2, 4, and 5 of the main body of the book are written by Wengert.

Gordon Lathrop comes to the discussion from the point of view of liturgical studies. He investigates, first of all, the current importance of the word "assembly" for liturgical renewal. He then reflects on a variety of ways that the marks of the church might be important to actual liturgical planning and current liturgical meaning in the churches, proposing that such a list of marks could be of great value in discussions between bishops—or other "visitors"—and their congregations. Chapters 1, 3, and 6 of the book are written by Lathrop.

The book concludes with each writer reflecting on what the other has said. One of the most important characteristics of this book is the side-by-side work of a liturgical theologian and a Reformation historian, both of whom have had their own particular voices in other contexts. We hope to model listening and cooperation as key theological virtues, virtues that do not need to imply any diminishing of the sharpness of the point. The appendixes contain documents important to the historical argument.

This book had its origin in four realities. First, Timothy Wengert has long been at work on detailed and contextual examination of key theological *loci* in the Reformation. His search for the origins of the idea of the marks of the church was an obvious outgrowth of these examinations. Second, Gordon Lathrop has written extensively about the importance and centrality of "the means of grace"—one way to discuss the marks of the church—in liturgical reform and renewal. Third, Lathrop and Wengert—we—have served together for more than a decade at the Lutheran Theological Seminary at Philadelphia, and that school has provided us with a place for our own dialogue about these matters. And, finally, we were together invited by the bishops of the ELCA to give a series of lectures to their annual Academy in January 2001. Those lectures have become this book.

So, with deep thanks to the bishops and to our common place of teaching, with more thanks than we can say to the persons to whom this book is dedicated, and with an invitation to you, dear reader, to join in the conversation, we turn together to the marks of the church. How *do* you know the Christian church when you encounter it?

Gordon W. Lathrop and Timothy J. Wengert
Holy Cross Day, 2003

Part One

Marks

Chapter 1

Church Is Assembly

"Show me deare Christ, thy Spouse, so bright and clear," calls out the seventeenth-century poet John Donne in one of his "Holy Sonnets," expressing an agonizing search.[1] "But how will or how can a poor confused person tell where such Christian holy people are to be found in this world?" asks Martin Luther, translating the phrase "holy catholic church" of the Apostles' Creed in his own unique way.[2]

Are these our questions? Do we, with Donne, search to find the authentic church in our own time? Do we, with Luther, ask about those manifest marks or notes by which God's own assembly may be known? Some of us may freely confess that these are living, urgent questions for us. Others might not put it quite like that. But, imagining the discussion in our own time, perhaps we may articulate the questions in these ways: Amid all of the pluralities and welcome diversities of these postmodern times, what unites Christians? Amid all the assemblies and communities in which we may take part, how do we recognize "the holy catholic church, the communion of saints," in which we may find, as the creed continues, "the forgiveness of sins"? What central and identifying matters ought one Christian congregation recognize and affirm in another Christian congregation? What absences in the one ought another admonish? What things should a bishop or superintendent or area leader look for, welcome, and support, and what things not, as that bishop cares for the church? Or to put the matter simply, in the language of ordinary people trying to organize their lives, How do I find a church I can trust?

And in asking these questions, how shall we begin?

3

Assembly in the Bible

Start with the Bible. Consider one important but little noticed biblical image, savoring it for a bit: In Nehemiah 8, the people who have
returned from the exile are pictured as having gathered in a great
assembly. It involves all of the people, from all the towns, "men and
women and all who could hear with understanding" (8:2). They are
gathered in a square before a gate in the newly restored wall of
Jerusalem, the gate that presumably opens from the city toward a
water-source, the Water Gate. They ask Ezra to bring the book of the
torah, and he does. Then, on a great wooden platform in their midst (a
migdal in Hebrew; a *bema,* the Greek of the Septuagint says) he opens
the book. The people all stand; Ezra blesses God; the people cry out,
"Amen, Amen," lifting up their hands in praise and bowing down in
adoration (v. 6); and Ezra reads to them. From early morning until
midday, he reads to them. He reads, and the Levites, scattered among
the people, perhaps, or taking turns on the *bema,* give the interpretation of the text. The people, long separated from this word, longing
for it, troubled by it, begin to mourn and weep. Ezra says:

> Go your way, eat the fat and drink sweet wine and send portions
> of them to those for whom nothing is prepared, for this day is
> holy to our LORD; and do not be grieved, for the joy of the LORD
> is your strength. (8:10)

And the assembly ends in just this way:

> And all the people went their way to eat and drink and to send
> portions and to make great rejoicing, because they had under-
> stood the words that were declared to them. (8:12)

This image of assembly—even in its details—evokes for us other biblical assemblies as well. At least two come to mind, both from primary and framing moments in the narratives of the Hebrew
scriptures. First, the people assemble at the foot of Sinai (Exodus
19–24). This is that very people which is to be "a priestly kingdom
and a holy nation" (19:6). Here, again, or first of all, is the *torah,* the
oral instruction, the lively word: from Moses they hear the very words
of God. And then the meal: they enter into the covenant, and in their

representatives, accompanying Moses on the mountain, they behold God and—far from being struck dead—they eat and drink (24:11).

Then, in the promises of the prophetic literature (e.g., Isaiah 2 and 25), all the nations are to be invited to such an assembly. The word of God, the *torah*, the holy instruction, will be sounded from "the mountain of the LORD's house" (2:2), to a gathering from all over the world. And the life-giving, comfort-giving meal will be there as well:

> On this mountain the LORD of hosts will make for all peoples a feast of rich food, a feast of well-aged wines. . . .The LORD will destroy on this mountain the shroud that is cast over all peoples . . .wiping away the tears from all faces." (25:6-8)

Like the assembly at the Water Gate, these biblically imaged gatherings—at the beginning of the vocation of Israel and at the end of time—have their center in the voice or word of God and their culmination in a shared and life-giving meal in which God is the primary host or source of strength. And if the people of Nehemiah's meeting pass through the desert from exile to come through the Water Gate to the square around the *bema,* then these other meetings are also constituted by great transitional journeys, the first people having passed through the sea, the final assembly made up as "all the nations stream" to God's mountain (Isa. 2:2). God's intentions with the world are declared in an assembly. And an assembly of people is made to be both God's priests for the sake of that world (Exod. 19:6) and an image of the final merciful goal for all.

In one place or another in the scriptures, all three of these gatherings are called by the same name: *qahal* or, in the Greek, *ekklesia,* "the meeting," "the assembly."[3] Unfolded by these stories, the name now can evoke in us a longing to sometime see such a meeting, hear its word, taste its food, know its life-giving gift. "Assembly," like many of the full-bodied images of the Hebrew scriptures, calls forth a strong response in us. Indeed, "assembly," described in such a way, is a "deep symbol"[4] in many of our cultures and sensibilities, though probably also a symbol that is endangered and effaced.

Of course, to find "word" and "meal" central to each of these accounts is to read the stories as a Christian. But the parallels between these various biblical assemblies are actually there in the texts. And

the power of the images does call up a modern longing. It is a longing that may hover about as we consider the power of such modern
gatherings as the town meeting or the march on Washington, the
Super Bowl or even the "virtual meetings" of the "chat-room," seen
against the continuing and widespread human longing for "authentic
community."

But that name—*ekklesia,* "the assembly"—has a further history. It
is the name that the early Christian communities called themselves,
the name we conventionally and somewhat opaquely translate as
"church." To translate a little more clearly, these communities were
"the assembly in the house of Nympha" (Col. 4:16) and "the meeting
of God that is in Corinth" (1 Cor. 1:1) and "all the assemblies of the
Gentiles" (Rom. 16:4) and even, somehow, considered as a *whole,* "the
assembly of God" (Gal. 1:13) throughout the world.[5] It is quite possible that this early Christian name was intended to evoke the
Hebrew scriptural "assembly," and not just to function as a Christian
use of the antique Hellenic term for the voters' gathering of all the
free males in a Greek city. The remarkable description of a Christian
gathering in Heb. 12:18-24 suggests as much. So does the famous
application to a Christian gathering of the Sinai imagery for the
assembled people: "You are a chosen race, a royal priesthood, a holy
nation, God's own people," says 1 Peter (2:9).[6] The Christian assembly was not just any gathering. The early Christians did not seem to
use for themselves the name that some of their opponents could apply.
They were not a "club" or an "association," *hetairia* as Pliny would
say.[7] They were *ekklesia.* It can be argued that the name intends a
gathering seen as being in continuity with Sinai and the Water Gate.
Or, to say the matter in another way, the word *ekklesia* may well have
been available precisely because some of the central marks of those old
stories were seen as present also in the Christian meeting: God acting,
the peoples gathering, the word proclaimed, a meal held, portions
sent.

Only in early Christian use there was a difference. The deep symbol was reoriented, broken to a new purpose. The gathering now was
not at Sinai nor at Jerusalem—"neither on this mountain nor in
Jerusalem," the Johannine Jesus says (John 4:21)—but in every local
place where at least a few people gathered, usually in houses slowly

being transformed for this purpose.[8] And the gathering was no longer
an ideal image, occupying a place in inexpressible hope or ancient
myth. Rather, the *ekklesia* was real folk, here, now. Like the Isaian
image, according to this early Christian linguistic use, the nations
were indeed beginning to stream together to hear God's word. Like
all three biblical assemblies, the scriptures were read in these meetings and interpreted. The word of God gave the meeting a center,
made it something other than a club, gave it a reason for the open
door to the arriving nations. And a meal was held in every Sunday
gathering, as seal and sign and presence of that life-giving word. At
least, that is the case when we can begin to discern the contents of the
Christian meeting, in Luke 24 and Acts 20, for example, or later in
the writings of Justin. And, if we can believe Paul (1 Cor. 16:2) and
then Justin, portions were also being sent from the Sunday assembly
to "those for whom nothing is prepared":

> Those who are prosperous and who desire to do so, give what
> they wish, according to each one's own choice, and the collec-
> tion is deposited with the presider. He aids orphans and wid-
> ows, those who are in want through disease or through another
> cause, those who are in prison, and foreigners who are sojourn-
> ing here.[9]

But this end-time assembly had a radically new content. One way
to say it is this: It is to the death and resurrection of Jesus Christ that
the nations are being gathered. The last day of God has begun. The
assembly of God, celebrating the new exodus, the new return from
exile for all the earth, is already now gathering the nations wherever
the word and meal that bear witness to the life-giving meaning of
Jesus' death are taking place. The scriptures are read with his death in
mind, and his resurrection has become the content of the "instruction" going out to the nations. The Triune God is present in the reading and the preaching, just as God was present in the text read at the
Water Gate, in the voice at Sinai, in the word going forth from Zion
at the end. And God is the host of the meal, setting out rich food for
the poor by the power of the Spirit. These gatherings are about the
meaning of the world before God, in God's judgment, under God's
mercy. Their participants are just folks, marked with many of the

signs of mortality and sin, of local inequities and local needs. But the word and meal at the center of the gathering promise justice and the end of tears. The food and money and words that are then sent into the streets bear witness to the dawning presence of that promise. And there is even a way to come into this meeting, to become part of the assembly-before-God. Baptism, its communal process and its water, evoke the passage through the sea and through the desert; the nations are now streaming through the Water Gate. In the images of that assembly as we see them in Acts 2, or Acts 20, or Luke 24, or John 20, or the mid-second-century account of Justin, the gathering called church has certain strong, central characteristics.

Catholic Churches in a Pluralistic Age

Can we leap from that early time to this? Can we set the biblical symbol within our own pluralistic age? One might try to say it this way:

These things are *catholic,* universal, found throughout God's world: a local assembly of people, constituted by baptism, participating together in the word and meal that, by the power of the Spirit, draw them into God's intention for all the world in Jesus Christ, in communion with other such assemblies in other places, inheriting the ancient Christian use of the assembly-image of the scriptures. By this conception, each assembly in each place is the catholic *ekklesia,* as it stays centered in these things. Locality and particularity belong to the essence of this catholicity. The catholic church is not a massive institution with a powerful central headquarters. Nor is it an ideal reality, somewhere else. It is always a local meeting, local people using local language, locally prepared food, local water sources. But it is always a local meeting gathered before and enlivened by the one God. Its words, food, and water are used with biblical and Christian eschatological intent. And, because God is the central actor here, this local assembly will always be itself opening onto and participating in the one assembly of God of every time and every place.

So, if it is indeed the assembly of God, this gathering will seek to send and receive signs of its communion with the other assemblies.[10] It will break open any tendency to let locality, local culture, turn in upon itself. Indeed, patterns and books for the local use of words and meal and bath anciently circulated as signs of communion between assemblies. The very collection of biblical books itself was first of all such a sign of communion. Then the churches have exercised further such signs: mutual affirmation and admonition in the use of these central things according to the deep intention of the meeting (church orders, creeds, and conciliar decisions being forms of such affirmation and admonition) and mutual recognition of the persons who lead (the slow development of diverse patterns of ministry being rooted in a search for such recognition).

But note: church, catholic church, is always *assembly*. The Bible is a book for the assembly. Bishops are local presiders in an assembly or, later, visitors in the many assemblies of a city or region, a sign of their unity, calling for the wider communion of assemblies. Creeds are the confessions of an assembly in communion with other assemblies and the confession of the baptized as they join that assembly and that communion.

Of course, these assertions about what is catholic have been made by a kind of "sorting." These are current assertions, made in the midst of present need, at the beginning of the twenty-first century, and made, one hopes, with informed awareness of history and an evangelical turn to present times. In doing such sorting, we probably ought to set aside the famous "canon" of the fifth-century semi-Pelagian Vincent of Lérins: that is catholic, he said, which was believed everywhere, always and by everyone. It seems unlikely that such universal belief can ever be established. We might more confidently hold with the more modest proposal of the fifth-century Augustinian Prosper of Aquitane: the rule of beseeching—the urging of the apostle (in 1 Tim. 2:1) that prayers should be made for everyone and the widespread response of the churches in actually doing that—establishes the rule of believing. The catholic faith is that everyone needs God and God's grace.[11] The catholic practice is to make that witness, to hold an open assembly, to pray—in the assembly—for everyone, and to welcome as many as will come to the assembly's signs of God's grace. The catholic church is an open, public assembly, not a club, not a *collegium* of the like-minded. Then, *catholic* is not so much a name for what is actually everywhere but for a simple practice that ought to be everywhere, that is indeed always struggling to come to expression everywhere, that is God's gift to everyone.

So we sort. We do so like other people in the history of the church who have sorted—Luther, for example—"holding fast to what is good."[12] Is assembly good? The catholic assembly is a participating people gathered around word, table, bath as a way to be immersed in the very presence of God. Shall we do that? Why should we do that? Is "assembly" really necessary for us to be Christian? Is it a useful thing to our actual common life in the present time? Does it not seem rather like an odd remnant from other cultural times, a longing vaguely awakened by old stories?

These somewhat jarring questions, of course, arise from our context. But, paradoxically, if the catholic assembly is always local, then we always need to take our context into serious consideration, even if that context raises questions about assembly itself. So what can we say about our context that may illuminate why "assembly" may indeed be a deep symbol for us, a symbol worthy of recovery, while it may also be a threatened or effaced symbol?

The libraries are full of books—and the internet is full of "postings"—that mean to examine thoroughly our postmodern, multicultural context. While this book cannot review all of these analyses, one major social study we should recall proposes that North America currently suffers from a serious decline in "social capital."[13] That is to say, our common life is marked by a lessening and deterioration of those public and communal institutions where we mix with a wide company of people—people other than close family or fellow employees—building trust, conversing, volunteering, creating civic networks. But note: it is not simply mainline church attendance that has suffered reverses. So have PTAs and book clubs and bowling leagues! We still bowl, for example, but we bowl alone, not in leagues. The study, called, in fact, "Bowling Alone," offers a variety of possible reasons for this decline: weariness with public engagement and public hope after a century of horrors; the astronomical increase in the salaried employment of women, who had been the traditional backbone of much voluntarism; the general shift to an ethic of self-realization and entertainment; the difficulty at finding common values amid burgeoning multiculturality. But, finally, the scholarship of "Bowling Alone" points to one major source of this decline: the presence of "virtual community" in our living rooms and on our computer screens. The sense of engagement with others has become available to us through laugh tracks, "you are there" sporting events, the personable pitches of shopping channels, the television preachers saying, "God loves you and so do I," the "chat rooms," even the exchange of virtual identities. And this engagement does not require commitment. It does not even require leaving the place of our own glowing screens. We soar into the crowded virtual population of cyberspace, but we seem to leave our own sad flesh, and its actual networks of connection, behind.

To be sure, the television screen, the multiplication of cable channels, and the internet are *tools,* not the enemy. They are tools, not unlike the telephone or the radio, perhaps even like the camera and the printing press, and they can, indisputably, be used for the well-being of our commonwealth. The very proliferation of options they enable may be linked to the classic American values of democracy and individualism and local control. Still, we probably ought not leap so quickly to the conclusion, common for some commentators, that we are in the midst of a major paradigm shift in the definition of the human being. And we ought to note that for a people who imagine that we are always reinventing ourselves, it is astonishing to see how likely we are to being invented by someone else, to stories received uncritically from the television, and to fads or even demagogues on the net. The point here, however, is that, according to the "Bowling Alone" study, "community," even a kind of "assembly," does still strongly figure in our symbolic universe, even if it is only assembly of the "virtual" kind. Indeed, some commentators note that any leading characteristic which is noted in the American popular culture—say, "bowling alone"—needs always to be immediately paired with its shadow side, its opposite—say, our nearly universal longing for genuine community. (The current undertaker, for example, may be saying, "I help people develop their *own* rituals." The shadow side of that assertion is the longing for some authentic, meaningful, and deeply traditional ritual, a longing represented by the fact that the undertaker may be drawing on Tibetan or Native American or Quaker sources, as he helps people craft "their own" rituals.)

We also ought be careful about too quickly joining those who assert that a people subject to such technological devices is a people without "culture."[14] That is, they are a people without shared deep symbols, except as these survive in marginal groups, whose gatherings are often powered by a need to resist the dominant culture. No, it is probably wiser to recognize that longings for the deep symbol *assembly* do survive among all of us, and that they not infrequently break out in something more than a virtual way—in rallies and rock concerts, in parades and even the rare town meeting, in vigorous hopes for schools and workplaces to exhibit communal spirit—though these manifestations may find it difficult to give us both a sense of community and a sense of the treasured importance of each person. Furthermore, if culture is that body of enacted symbolic material that enables a people to live together in a land,[15] then, with or without technological devices, we too have stories we live by (even if they are only the narratives of television advertisements), ways of sharing food (even if we simply share a common refrigerator on the run), a set of value-carrying common symbols (even if our community is primarily virtual), and rituals (even if someone sells us his ability to help us to craft our own). These may be our ways of "living in the land," even when those ways are primarily patterns of consumerism, purchasing for the self—even purchasing rituals for the self—being then the primary form of "life."

No, it is wiser to acknowledge that culture is always a collective disagreement, marked with manifest as well as hidden tensions.[16] We consumers know vaguely, sometimes sharply, that purchasing is not very satisfactory as a primary form of interaction with the land. We are aware that many people among us are poor enough or alienated enough to have little role in the consumerist patterns for living. We do newly sense that our own invention of local rituals, our practice of "God decentralized,"[17] may be an important step toward living in the land together. But when the most real resources we can find for our religious practice are in web postings, we must admit that the glowing screen finally gives cold comfort to the longing for community. The screen may give us a kind of "assembly." It may tell us stories to live by. But it cannot give us a real, shared meal, except in the sad but widespread parody of overeating junk food alone before the screen. And it cannot enable us genuinely to send portions to those for whom nothing is prepared.

Receiving Assembly Again

We can offer each other better, deeper cultural practices, practices that enable us to live more fully and meaningfully with each other in the land, than can be possible with these device-determined fulfillments of our symbolic longings. And our "sad flesh" does not need to be left behind as we exercise our hunger for deep symbols in our flights into virtual identity. Our flesh—we—can come into a real meeting, a meeting that cares profoundly about our common existence together in the flesh, in the flesh beloved of God. We can propose that we try the recovered practice of the Christian deep symbol *assembly*.

It will take some recovery. We have had "going to church." Subtly, gradually, our gatherings have become a kind of religious consumerism, as well. We have come together to the ministrations of the expert religious professional. We have purchased such ministrations as we decided that we needed for ourselves, chosen the place of our purchases according to our own taste in music, ritual, or rhetoric. It is no wonder that anxiety about the results of "bowling alone" in our church attendance has led some of us to heighten the consumerist appeals to the "market." And it is no wonder that people searching for a genuinely religious alternative to the consumerist patterns turn away from the churches as being too little spiritual, too little "other," searching instead in the religious cultures of oppressed or marginalized or exotic peoples. Perhaps, indeed, in older times, a full community-life around "going to church" provided constant reinforcement to Christianity as a way of life, but now that fuller community life is gone, if it was ever there. Now we have going to church, sometimes.

Let us, then, recover assembly, keep assembly, and honor and love the assembly. Why? To start with, because making up our own private rituals is singularly unsatisfying. All we will meet in them, finally, is our own untranscendent selves. If our cultural situation requires of us that we engage in the marketplace, then let us set out amid the commerce of our cities the free and communal bread of grace—the surprising commerce of God's blessedness given freely in exchange for our wretchedness and inviting us to turn toward the needs of our neighbor[18]—rather than the stone of the lonely self, the only *virtually* accompanied and thus still lonely self. Ancient—even exotic—wisdom, after all, is available within the Christian tradition. Christians believe that those ancient assemblies, their shape, their intention, their word, their meal, their portions for the hungry, are our heritage and gift in the local *ekklesia*. And the central matters of the assembly, the central matters of catholic worship—stories to live by, an important communal meal, the establishment of our identity in baptism—are stunningly relevant to daily North American life, to a people in quest of identity, nostalgic for communal and meaningful meals, searching for worthy stories to live by.

What do we mean here by "assembly?" We mean a fully participating gathering, manifestly and strongly centered, every Sunday, around the reading and preaching of scripture as Book of Life, the celebration of the Lord's Supper as the life-giving meal par excellence, and the sending of food and help "to those for whom nothing is prepared." We mean such a gathering constituted by baptism, remembering baptism, and singing and praying around the central matters of word and sacrament. We mean a gathering with such a strong center, but also with very open doors, with a very permeable exterior boundary, with a strong welcome to "strangers." We mean such an assembly understanding itself as in communion with all of the churches of God throughout the earth and throughout time, all of them constituting together a single assembly. Communion with other assemblies, an open door as to a public event, the great bath as a way to come in, and, at the center, word and table and sending to the poor: these things are a beginning list of some "marks of the church."

"Assembly" is the most basic symbol used by Christian worship. And the renewed practice of "assembly" is probably the primary need for any authentic liturgical renewal in our current cultural context.[19] It is not by accident that the word "assembly" is repeatedly used in the descriptions and proposals of the ELCA statement on "the use of the means of grace,"[20] since those very means have their home in and give a center to assemblies.

Indeed, "assembly" can engage and respond to current pluralistic American culture in deeply important ways. Assembly, in the sense used here, can release us from the perpetual need to invent ourselves, inviting us rather to be a people formed by the Spirit in identity with Jesus Christ, who identifies with all the hungry and the godless, and thus to be a people standing before the living God. At the same time, assembly can reflect the deep current longing for the decentralized: catholic church is always profoundly local assembly. It is never appropriately a local office representing headquarters somewhere else, though it is indeed—and very helpfully—local assembly sending and receiving signs of communion with all the other assemblies and with a meaning that is also more than local. So local ways—diverse cultural ways—to gather, speak, sing, eat, and drink will all be important as long as it is the central *ekklesia*-business they are doing. And assembly can appropriately reflect something of democratic values: all the people are welcome to participate; each one is honored; many ministers represent and serve the people; and therefore there is a resistance to making a single charismatic leader the center of the meeting.

And, perhaps in the most important connection to current culture, assembly can receive our longing for community, but criticize it, invite it to transformation. Here is a "community" that has the central matters of God's gift in common, not our quest for immediate access to the other.[21] Here is a strongly local gathering that has a continual impulse toward the more-than-local at its heart. Here is a meeting where the leaders are frequently from elsewhere and always in communion with a larger reality, as large as possible a reality. Here is a community where one who is in the very middle of the meeting— Jesus Christ, who identifies with all outsiders—constantly criticizes and breaks down any boundary around the community. Here is a gathering where sending portions to those for whom nothing is prepared belongs to the essence of the gathering.

Such an assembly, as both gift and task for our local congregations, will need to occur without much support from our current culture. Even though "assembly" stands in dialogue with the values and deep symbols of our cultural moment, it is also strange, unknown, and rare. At the same time, such an assembly will need to avoid attempts of withdrawal from cultural engagement, as if it were a community of resident aliens. Just as its biblical stories of grace amid death and life are a transformation of our hopes for stories to live by, and just as its meals and its sending of portions are a critique and transformation of both our meal-keeping and our economy, so also the gathering around these things receives our hope for community, brings that hope under criticism, and offers us a beginning of our cultural hopes transformed.

But such an assembly will be helped by the encouragement and love and teaching of its bishop, as that bishop continues to understand, imagine, teach, and proclaim what church actually is. And such an assembly will be helped by a relationship of mutual affirmation and admonition with other assemblies.

Here is a beginning for a current Christian: Love your own assembly. See it as Sinai, the Water Gate, Mount Zion drawing the nations. See it as the very place where the grace of our Lord Jesus Christ and the love of God actually are dwelling amid the communion—this very concrete communion—of the Holy Spirit.[22] Believe what the word of greeting at the outset of the liturgy says. Do not be afraid. Help the assembly stay strongly centered on the central matters, on the book and the meal and the sending to the hungry, not on our own menu of tastes in music or style, not on the charismatic leader or the charismatic band or the charismatic organ, not on whatever clichés we may have for "going to church." Help the assembly open its doors. Help it welcome everyone, old hand and the newest inquirer alike, to the dignity of being a participant in the assembly of God.

Then, we need to go on to consider whether these assertions about the current relevance of a New Testament conception of *ekklesia* have any connection with the classic lists of the marks of the church. And we need to consider where such an idea of marks of the church even came from. But that will take at least another chapter.

Chapter 2

A Brief History of the
Marks of the Church

The Mystery

Historians love mysteries. That is, in part, what so attracts them to history in the first place. They will spend hours tracking down the origin of a passage, discovering a new manuscript or publication, or identifying the date of a letter or the source of an idea. Inquiring after the origins of the "marks of the church," presents a historical mystery par excellence. Where did the concept of "marks of the church" (in Latin, *notae ecclesiae*) first arise? Providing an answer to that question will provide new avenues for understanding the church in the present and unlock the heart of a Lutheran ecclesiology.

If we ask from what source Martin Luther borrowed the notion of the *notae ecclesiae,* the scholarly literature is strangely silent.[1] Even the standard texts on Luther's ecclesiology do not raise this question.[2] Broader surveys of Luther's theology acknowledge the importance of the term but give little hint as to its origin.[3] In short, answering this question will involve more than repeating a standard source of past research. There is next to nothing to consult!

At first glance, the *Oxford Dictionary of the Christian Church* seems to offer some help.[4] In this case, however, the *Dictionary* proves to contain not simply disappointment but out-and-out distortion. In an entry entitled, "Notes of the Church," which in its peculiar rendering of the Latin terms already raises suspicions, the author claims that the first enumeration occurred in the Nicene Creed: "one, holy, catholic, and apostolic." This claim is historically misleading, if for no other reason than that no commentator in the first 1,500 years of the

17

church's history ever called those four adjectives "marks" of the church. In fact, the author of the article admits as much by mentioning in passing that no theologian had commented upon them until the Reformation, when Roman Catholic theologians used them "to discern the true Church among the rival claims of the different Christian Communions."

The article also pointed out (correctly) that treatises on the marks of the church became particularly abundant in the mid-sixteenth century. What puzzled the writer, however, was that these lists of marks were not confined to the Nicene Creed's four. In fact, Robert Bellarmine, the seventeenth-century Roman Catholic defender of the Council of Trent, had enumerated fifteen. The author of the *Oxford Dictionary*'s article hastened to add (incorrectly) that Bellarmine's list is ultimately reducible to the four. In the nineteenth century, the author adds, the English Tractarians—that group dedicated to revitalizing the Church of England through a return to its pre-Reformation roots—used these four to prove Anglican catholicity. This reference indicates that the author has turned the history on its head in an effort to allow for the term in its High-Church Anglican construal of the nineteenth century and at the same time to downplay the Reformation's role in the debate. That is, nineteenth-century English theologians among others applied the term "marks of the church" to the Nicene Creed. Before that, the term had a very different meaning.

It is easy enough to call into question the *Dictionary*'s disinformation simply by examining an excerpt of the seventeenth-century debate. Cardinal Bellarmine did write extensively on the question of the *notae ecclesiae,* but not in a vacuum. He was responding to the cornerstone of evangelical ecclesiology that went to the very heart of the difference between Wittenberg and Rome. If Bellarmine could show that his understanding of the church's marks were correct, then he could at the same time prove that Rome was that church and that the evangelical churches were not churches at all. Of course, such an argument could not go unchallenged. In this case, the seventeenth century's foremost Lutheran orthodox theologian, John Gerhard, stepped up and, in his massive *Loci communes theologici,* refuted all fifteen marks proposed by Bellarmine, putting in their stead a Lutheran list. These hundreds of pages of refutation formed almost the entire theological locus on the church![5]

This, however, does not finally answer the question of the term's origins, especially in Luther. For that, historians may turn to one of the most useful tools in Luther research: the Latin index to the Weimar edition of Luther's works (the German index is not yet published). There, surprisingly, the term rarely comes up. To be sure, Luther uses the *concept* but only on rare occasions the term itself, *notae ecclesiae,* marks of the church. Not to find clear indication that Luther knew or used the term consistently—much less that he understood it as a technical term or theological jargon (the way theologians use it today)— was like Sherlock Holmes's discovery of the dog that did not bark.

The Terms of the Solution

Luther's disuse of the term may provide an answer to the mystery. Martin Luther himself developed the concept and on occasion used the term *notae ecclesiae* to describe it. When someone close to Luther— Philip Melanchthon (1497–1560)—used and explained the phrase in the 1531 Apology of the Augsburg Confession, it quickly became a technical term and was caught up in the growing ecclesiological debate of the 1530s.[6] This means that the marks of the church were central to how Luther and his successors understood church. Far from being a secret weapon stuck into the Nicene Creed and not discovered until centuries later, the marks of the church arose in a very specific polemical situation where Luther's opponents forced him to reevaluate his ecclesiology along evangelical lines. That is to say, the marks of the church, rightly understood, are part and parcel of Luther's Reformation breakthrough: that we are justified by faith alone without the works of the law.

In the earliest texts, Luther most often used the word *signa* or signs of the church. He argued that we can tell where the church is because God has given certain signs, especially baptism, the Lord's Supper, and the preached word of God.[7] Of course, the word *signum* had a rich and honored history among Latin-speaking theologians. They had used it in at least two ways. First, borrowing terms from Neoplatonic hermeneutics, already Augustine had distinguished between *signum* and *res* in a scriptural text, that is, between the sign (the word or story in the text) and the spiritual reality *(res)* hidden in the text.[8] Second, again as part of the Augustinian tradition, theologians had often talked about the sacramental signs or actions that included the water of baptism and the bread and wine of the Lord's Supper.

The only reference to "signs" of the church before Luther came in connection to the Hussites and a debate at the Council of Basel in 1431. A treatise on the church by Johannes de Ragusa, which survived in two manuscripts and was not published until the twentieth century, refuted the spiritualized views on the church of John Wycliffe and Jan Hus.[9] In this connection, Ragusa used a single reference in Augustine's polemics against the Manichaeans, which Augustine intended as demonstrations of the church's authority.[10] According to Ragusa, Augustine[11] had defined five "signs and most certain indices" of the church: its most sincere wisdom and integrity of faith, the consent of the peoples and nations, the authority inaugurated by miracles, the succession of priests in the Petrine see, and the name "catholic church."[12] Of course, Ragusa, a late-medieval Dominican, was arguing that already for Augustine obedience to the papacy supplied the most important mark of all. Moreover, his point was to use such signs to *exclude* the Hussites and to champion the particular power arrangements of the late-medieval papacy. Similar claims were developed by John of Torquemada.[13] Again, the point was to defend the papacy and to prove that the Hussites were *not* the church and that the council was not over the pope.

Even though these arguments were most likely not known to those participating in the sixteenth-century debate, from the beginning the question was not whether there were marks of the church but what they were. Moreover, Luther's expressed comments demonstrated that he wanted no part of Wycliffe's or Hus's ecclesiologies. He was instead developing a peculiar, *inclusive* way to define church that embraced all Christians under the word and sacraments.

Luther was probably unfamiliar with these specific arguments. Nevertheless, it would seem at very least that the other technical uses of the term *signum* provided Luther with a convenient way to describe how to detect the church in the world. Although Luther did not yet employ the term *notae* for this concept, this word, too, had a technical meaning. This becomes clear, for example, from Thomas Aquinas's writings. The exhaustive *Index Thomisticus* proves that the angelic doctor never used the phrase *notae ecclesiae*. However, in one instance, in his Commentary on Boethius (the fifth-century Aristotelian philosopher and Christian) Thomas did make the point that whereas abstract concepts employ mathematical terms, sensible things have *notae*.[14] In Latin, the word *nota,* from which the English word "note" derives, comes from the past participle of the verb "to know." Thus, Thomas was making the philosophical distinction that people express abstract entities using abstract, mathematical terms. In contrast, sensible things have certain *notae,* that is, markings or characteristics by which they are known.

It would seem that Martin Luther and Philip Melanchthon, both of whom were well acquainted with Aristotelian philosophical terms, occasionally applied the term *notae* to this concept in Luther's theology, in part perhaps because *signum* connoted such a variety of things. Indeed, one of the earliest uses in a "public" document came in the Apology of the Augsburg Confession, VII.20.[15] Melanchthon called the word and sacraments the characteristic markings *(notae)* of the church. Perhaps Melanchthon employed this term rather than *signa,* because people could construe the latter to mean signs for an absent reality.[16] In English, one could properly use the phrase "signs of the church," as long as there was agreement that it meant something like "signs of life." In that case the sign (e.g., breathing) and the thing signified (life) are not absent from one another but very much together.[17]

Origins in Luther's Writings

Never underestimate the influence of Luther's opponents! They very often saw where his theology was heading long before he himself did. Luther occasionally admitted as much. For example, in the preface to the first volume of his German writings, published in 1539, he provided a short interpretation of Psalm 119. He noted that the psalmist

> so often in this psalm laments concerning the enemies, the wicked princes and tyrants, the lying and godless spirits, which he must suffer by reason of the very fact that he meditates, that he applies himself to God's Word, as we have said. For as soon

as God's Word goes forth through you the devil will afflict you
and make you a real doctor [of theology] and teach you by his
assaults to seek and to love God's Word. For I myself . . . must
be very thankful to my papists for pummeling, pressing, and
terrifying me; that is, for making me a fairly good theologian,
for otherwise I would not have become one.[18]

In the case of the marks of the church, Luther suffered in 1520–21
the twin pummeling of Ambrose Catharinus[19] (1484–1553) and
Thomas Murner (1475–1537). Catharinus was an Italian theologian
associated with the papal court. His fellow Italian and the official
papal court theologian, Sylvester Prierias (1456–1523), had written
the first official Roman response to Luther's Ninety-five Theses and
their defense. Luther had in turn written a refutation of Prierias's
work, to which Catharinus fashioned a reply. Thomas Murner was a
humanist living in Strasbourg who wrote several tracts against
Luther, especially attacking the *Babylonian Captivity of the Church*.
Luther responded in a brief appendix to a tract addressed primarily to
Jerome Emser.[20] In it, Luther consistently spelled Murner's name
with an "a" instead of an "e," thereby changing the last syllable of his
name to "*nar*," German for fool.

In fact, neither man was a fool. Their probing questions forced
Luther to articulate an ecclesiology based not upon Roman authority
but upon the gospel. As far as this historian can determine, Luther's
reply to Catharinus contains his earliest full exposition of the concept
later termed marks of the church.[21] Close examination of this single,
highly significant historical text may open the way to a renewed
appreciation for the peculiar evangelical (Lutheran) concern for the
marks of the church and how they may provide help for Christians
today.

Although Luther's first reference to the external signs of the church
(defined as the gospel, baptism, and the Lord's Supper) in his attack
on the Roman papacy against Augustine Alveld only mentions the
matter in passing, it may still contribute something to the origins of
the term. Alveld had tried to tar Luther with the brush of Jan Hus's
spiritualized ecclesiology. Luther, simply dismissed Alveld's claim.
Whether he was familiar with the criticisms of Jan Hus by Johannes

de Ragusa is doubtful. In any case, Luther insisted that the church had external signs.

Ambrose Catharinus's Challenge: Ecclesiological Absurdity
When the papal court theologian, Sylvester Prierias, took one look at Luther's Ninety-five Theses and their defense, he immediately saw a glaring weakness. Thus, at the beginning of his attack on Luther, he listed what theologians today would call his hermeneutical presuppositions, all four of which concerned papal primacy.[22] Luther responded in kind, not only discussing his method but also defining, in the course of his argument, the nature of the church. The church was comprised not of those who adhered to the pope but of those who trusted in Christ's promise of salvation. It was this comment that attracted the attention of Prierias's defender, Catharinus. In his tract, he wrote, "If the whole church is 'in the Spirit' and its reality completely spiritual, then no one could know where any part of it is in the whole world, which is absolutely absurd."[23]

This was no small challenge. Catharinus realized that if Luther's definition of church as the assembly of believers remained unchallenged, there were no grounds upon which to defend the primacy and authority of the papacy. He also constructed a masterful argument to use against Luther. Luther, in his opinion, had removed the church from this world and reduced it to an absurdity. People would never know whether they belonged to the church or not. The certainty of God's promise, so central for Luther's understanding of justification, had in Catharinus's view been rendered uncertain by an ecclesiology lacking any guarantors for God's promise. In response, Luther developed a highly nuanced and, quite frankly, unique approach to the question of church—an approach that remains undervalued or, at least in its original form, nearly unread by Lutheran, let alone other Christian theologians. The tract itself has never even been translated into English or modern German.

There are three ways today in which other churches and their theologians attack Luther's understanding of church as the assembly of believers. Some actually do accept Catharinus's construal and make the church entirely spiritual. These days, this comprises one of the attractions of "New Age" spirituality, which severs the connection between the gathering of the baptized believers around word and sacraments and the work of God. This is nothing short of the cult of the individual and, in trying to be completely spiritual, becomes instead completely solipsistic. The second way represents a variety of "papalist" positions. These folks say that there is a place and a person, which determine where the church is: whether that is Rome and the pope, Canterbury and the archbishop, Wittenberg and Luther, Geneva and Calvin—you name it. Luther attacked the sixteenth-century version of this notion without mercy. Finally, a variation of this second position points to the local pastor and congregation as the guarantor of church and gospel. Here, the appeal is less to historical continuity (although that occurs, too!) than to some sort of moral or doctrinal purity. In the search for pure guarantors of ministerial authority, these folks often revive a Donatist ecclesiology.[24] Pure pastors and their pure congregations represent the pure church—a particularly destructive notion when either pastor or congregation fails to live up to its expectations. Not surprisingly, similar sixteenth-century groups come under heavy attack in the Augsburg Confession (article VIII).

Luther's Response
1. The church and the incarnation: "In but not of"
Luther quoted the section of Catharinus's tract cited above and responded by attacking the papalism implied in his opponent's argument. The church is not about the see at Rome or the person of the pope. That is, it is not about place or person. Luther (rightly) suspected that Catharinus's argument denied the incarnational principle of all Christian doctrine and life. Thus, he wrote:

> Although the church lives in the flesh, it does not live according to the flesh, as Paul says in Gal. 1:11 and 2 Cor. 10:3. . . . For Christ excludes every place when he says [Luke 17:20-21], "The kingdom of God does not come through observation, and they cannot say, 'Here it is,' or 'There it is.'" And, "Behold, the kingdom of God is among you." And Paul [Rom. 2:11] excludes everybody when he says, "There are no favorites with God." For just as the church is not without food and drink in this life, and

yet, according to Paul [Rom. 14:17], the kingdom of God is not food or drink, so there is no church without a place or a body, and yet place and body are not the church nor do they pertain to it.[25]

"In the world but not of the world." This well-known comment revolves around the incarnation itself: Christ *in* the world, *in* the flesh, *in* sin, *in* death but not *of* those things. Luther rejects the notion of a completely spiritualized church (it is *in* the flesh!) but refuses a completely politicized version as well (but not *of* the flesh).

Here Luther's comments get to the heart of modern confusion about the church. Most people want desperately a "Here it is" on which to fix faith. God proclaims instead a man hanging on a cross, that is, God in the last place anyone would reasonably look. God joins us to that one's death and resurrection through water and word and to his body and blood through bread and wine—a scandal! The alternatives to Luther's understanding of the church are always ecclesiologies of glory— attempts to nail the kingdom of God down to a "Here it is!"

Yet Luther was no Platonist; he was not talking about some spiritualized Cloud Cuckoo Land. The church is in the flesh, just not of the flesh. It has places and bodies (including Rome and Wittenberg; Pope Leo and Martin Luther), but it does not consist of those things. In the sticky question of church order, this means that the church will always have an order of one sort or another, but it does not consist in and cannot put its trust in that order. As soon as someone says that to be truly church and to deliver the gospel the church can only have a particular order—congregational, presbyteral, episcopal, you name it—then he or she is defining not church but anti-church.[26]

2. Necessity and indifference in Luther's ecclesiology

Therefore a particular bread, drink, or clothing is not necessary for the church or the faithful, although they cannot live in this age without bread, drink, or clothing, but all these things are free and indifferent. So it is not necessary to have a certain place and a certain person, although it is not possible to be without place or person. But these, too, are all indifferent and free. Every place fits for the Christian, and no place is necessary for the

Christian; every person can shepherd the Christian and no par-
ticular person who shepherds is necessary. For freedom of the
Spirit rules here, and that freedom makes all things indifferent.
Nothing corporeal or earth-bound whatever is necessary.[27]

Here Luther introduced the notion of *adiaphora,* as Melanchthon
came to nickname it. The term Luther used, *indifferentia,* indifferent
matters, is the Latin equivalent of the Greek term Melanchthon preferred. This word comes from Cicero and is an important Stoic ethical
category.[28] These were matters that were morally neither right nor
wrong in themselves. But here Luther was already using the term in a
theological and ecclesiological sense. When it comes to defining
church, place, time, person, dress, food, or drink are all indifferent (or
undifferentiated) matters.

When Luther came storming back from the Wartburg to Wittenberg in 1522, he fought with his colleague Andreas Bodenstein von
Karlstadt over precisely the same issue.[29] In the late Middle Ages,
many were calling for reform of the church, "in head and members,"
to use their favorite term, by which they meant a reform of church
hierarchy and practice. Karlstadt, too, assumed that that was the
proper definition of Reformation, except that now it would occur on
a smaller scale (in Wittenberg) and involve especially Communion
practices, images, and the like. However, for Luther, *all* of these
things were adiaphora. What truly mattered to him were the proclaimed and visible word and the weak and tender conscience that
receives it. Thus, he insisted on allowing Communion in one kind,
despite his own attacks against the practice and the command of
Jesus. Much to the dismay of some Protestants, this flexibility continued into the so-called Visitation Articles of 1528, the first official
church order of electoral Saxony.[30] It is not that such *indifferentia* are
inconsequential or unimportant—they are!—but that such things
cannot claim to be necessary for the life and salvation of the church.

3. Luther's own definition of church
Having excluded Catharinus's definition of true church as bound to a
particular place (Rome) and a particular person (the pope), Luther
now offered his own definition.

Therefore, by what *sign* may I recognize the church? For some *visible sign* must be given by which we may congregate together to hear the word of God. I reply that the *necessary sign* is what we also have, namely, baptism, the bread, and, most importantly of all, the gospel. These three are the *symbols, tokens,* and *character-istics* of Christians. Where you see baptism and the bread and the gospel—in any place whatsoever, with any persons whatso-ever—you may have no doubts that the church exists there.[31]

Here, nine years before the presentation of the Augsburg Confession, Luther expressed the complete Lutheran ecclesiology. It never really changed. It is rarely disputed by Lutheran theologians and remains something of a conundrum for other churches. I experienced the effects of this very definition at Easter 1981. My family and I were living in Tübingen, Germany, where a friend invited us to a Roman Catholic Easter Vigil service, where we heard a powerful witness of the resurrection: "Jesus Christ is risen, and that makes all the difference for our lives." The next morning, having been so excited by what they proclaimed in the small Roman Catholic church in that predominantly Lutheran town, my family and I climbed aboard a city bus and ventured to the downtown church, the *Stiftskirche* (Foundation Church), an imposing edifice built in the fifteenth century and Lutheran since 1534. Surely they would do Easter up proper. In fact, except for the hymns, there was no mention in the entire service that Jesus Christ had risen from the dead. The pastor preached on Jesus' word from the cross, "Today you will be with me in paradise," and claimed he could not even wish the congregation "Happy Easter" because the previous day police had beaten some students in Hamburg. Where was "church" that Easter? Where we heard proclaimed Christ crucified and risen again for us, not where the only word was political commentary on police brutality.

Church is not a noun; it is a verb, an event, or, to use the language of the sixties, a happening. The point of the church's marks is not to provide a definition of church for theologians, ecumenists, and other suspicious people but to point out the "sign . . . by which we may congregate." The point of the church's marks is always to gather people for the hearing, washing, and eating of God's word.

This is countercultural. Most of the folks who join congregations today say that they did it out of convenience, fellowship, or habit. They rarely can articulate the power of God's Holy Spirit to draw believers together through the word. Yet that stands at the heart of every church event, whether at a local, regional, national, or international level.

Note here, too, that Luther did not yet know what to call these things. He began by calling them a *signum*, or sign, twice using an adjective to clarify his meaning. Then, as a sure sign that he was heading into a new theological and terminological territory, he piled up three more names: symbols, tokens, and characteristics (*symbola, tesserae et caracteres*). What caused him suddenly to redefine church? It was being justified by faith alone. The justifying word of the gospel eliminates all other things as objects of our trust, including the structure of the church. To paraphrase a political slogan from a past campaign for the American presidency, for Luther when it comes to defining the church, "It's the *word,* stupid."

4. Luther's grounds for Christian unity: The *notae ecclesiae*

> For in these signs Christ wants us to agree [*concordare*], as Ephesians 4:5f. says: [721] "One faith, one baptism, one Lord." Where the same gospel is, there is the same faith, the same hope, the same love, the same Spirit, and, in truth, all things are the same. This is the unity of Spirit, which Paul commands us carefully to preserve—not a unity of place, person, things or bodies. But where you do not see the gospel (as we see in the synagogue of the papists and the Thomists), even if they baptize and eat at the altar, you may have no doubt that the church does not exist there—except among children and the unlettered. Instead, you may know that there is Babylon—full of witches, hairy beasts, hyenas, jackals and other monsters [Isaiah 13:21-22], that is, I am referring to our "distinguished teachers."[32]

The very thing that now seems to divide the church, namely, Luther's attack on our worship of place and person and his new definition of church, in fact provides a whole new way to understand church unity and concord. This means that where there is agreement in word and sacraments, Luther and those who employ his ecclesiology found no reason not to call the other party church in the full sense of the term. One needs no proper certification or history, only the gospel. However, this also means that church unity is something given through the events of word and sacrament, not something human beings do, achieve, or preserve. To be sure, there can, in addition, be unity in human structures and visible reconciliation among divided brothers and sisters, but such is not to be confused with true Christian unity that happens as a gift of the Holy Spirit working through word and sacraments.

There is also another aspect to this definition, and that is an exception Luther built into his polemic—"except among children and the unlettered." This means that even where leaders run amok in bad theology or practice, God protects the little ones, giving them baptism and the Supper and allowing them to hear the gospel even in the midst of bad preaching! This caveat prevented Luther from becoming a Donatist, that is, one who judges the reality of the church by the purity of its leaders. It also meant that even in the face of the worst possible theology Luther did not reject Christians from other communities of faith out-of-hand.

Here it seems that Luther contradicted himself. On the one hand, he argued that wherever one finds these *signa*, one finds church. On the other, he insisted that despite the presence of baptism and the Supper, his opponents were not church. The reason for this tension becomes clear in the following: insofar as the papal party lacks the gospel, it is not church.

5. The gospel as the special sign of church

> For, compared to the bread and baptism, the gospel is the unparalleled, most certain and noblest symbol of the church. For through the gospel alone it is conceived, formed, supported, born, educated, fed, clothed, adorned, strengthened, armed, preserved, in short, the whole life and substance of the church is in the word of God. As Christ says [Matt. 4:4]: "The human being lives from every word that proceeds from the mouth of God."[33]

Although this preeminence of the gospel suffered abuse at the hands of later Lutherans, it nevertheless prevents several dangers in the present church. First, there can be little doubt that later orthodox Lutherans transformed "gospel" into knowledge about God and "justification by faith alone" into justification by right answer alone. That Luther had something far more profound in mind is indicated by the string of verbs that reflect the stages of human life, beginning with conception. The gospel conceives, forms, supports, bears, educates, feeds, clothes, adorns, strengthens, arms, and preserves the church. One can argue in reverse and say that where the preaching and teaching are not doing these things, then the gospel itself is missing.

Here, in the second place, Luther admitted that the sacraments without explanation or proclamation cannot do their work among us.[34] Christians dare not reduce the sacraments to hocus-pocus, which does not strengthen and create faith. Imagine a baptism where no one says, "Timothy John, I baptize you in the name of the Father, and of the Son, and of the Holy Spirit," that is, where no one confesses the Triune God and pours that name over the child or adult with the water. Every morning Americans perform wordless "baptisms," but they are merely showers or baths. Imagine a Lord's Supper with simply "a loaf of bread, a jug of wine, and thou beside me in the wilderness." It may be a lovers' feast or an after-work snack at the bar, but without Christ and his promises, it will always be only our supper or their supper but never the Lord's Supper.

6. Defining the gospel

> I am not talking about a written gospel but a spoken one. Nor am I talking about the kind of oration declaimed in churches from a raised pulpit. I am talking about the pure and genuine word, which teaches true faith in Christ—not that "unformed," Thomistic kind of faith—and which, extinguished and suffocated through the pope and the papists, is now silenced throughout the world. For this reason, Christ demands nothing from the Apostles with such perseverance than that they spread the gospel.[35]

As Eric Gritsch once wrote, quoting Luther, "The Church is not a quill house but a mouth house."[36] Neither Luther nor the other authors in *The Book of Concord* defined the word of God as simply a book. Lutherans were never meant to be book worshipers. In the sixteenth century, with Reformers like Calvin and even Martin Bucer worried about the inspired text and with Romanists arguing over an inspired pope or council to interpret that inspired book, Luther had very different concerns. It is not the words in a book, but the proclamation on the lips that is for him most clearly word of God.

Moreover—and this is one of the few times Luther discussed this problem so forthrightly—he clearly did not mean just any old sermon, but especially one that proclaims a "pure and genuine word" and "teaches true faith in Christ." Luther was asking the preacher, "When you preach, what happens? Do you simply bore your audience? Share with them some interesting stories and enlightened exegesis? Entertain them?" That is what Luther was speaking against in no uncertain terms: rhetorically pleasing but theologically vacuous orations.

In other contexts, he went after other (nomian or antinomian) preachers, too. "When you preach, do you simply clobber your poor pastors with the law? Congratulate them on all their good works?"[37] "Or, as an antinomian preacher, do you try to wish the condemning, terrifying voice of the law away by," in Luther's actual words, "a play put on in an empty theater?"[38] That is, does the preacher pretend to do away with the threats of the law by mere sleight-of-hand? Luther was asking the preachers, "When you preach, do you simply cover up the realities of the human situation to such a degree that you describe sin as little more than a facial blemish rather than the terminal disease that it is?" Unless the preaching actually does the deed—that is, brings human beings to faith by telling them the truth about themselves (law) and about God's unending love for them in Christ (gospel)—in that order—then it is no more than fancy words from a raised pulpit.

7. Succession in evangelical ecclesiology
After having used the text in John 21 ("Feed my sheep") to prove the centrality of the gospel and after having rejected Catharinus's use of

the same text to bolster papal claims to domination, Luther contrasted the ministry of the gospel to power politics.

> Therefore these figments of papistic imagination must be condemned because the office of jurisdiction is one thing but the office of brotherly love is another. The gospel and the church are ignorant of jurisdictions, which are nothing more than the tyrannical inventions of human beings. It knows only love and service, not power and tyranny. Therefore, whoever teaches the Gospel is pope, Peter's successor. Whoever does not is Judas, Christ's traitor.[39]

Here Luther described precisely how many people sin against today's (evangelical) bishops, pastors, and other church leaders by refusing to recognize that theirs is not an office of jurisdiction but of love and service. The temptation is to make too much of the order it takes to run an organization while forgetting the gospel itself. We know only one thing as human beings apart from God, and that is to worry about jurisdiction. This concern is fine for this world; it is fine for the ordering of the church. However, it has nothing directly to do with the gospel. The gospel knows only of love and service. That is why the preferred name for ordained priests or pastors among sixteenth-century Lutherans was "minister"—Latin for "servant." Christians know the one who was numbered with the transgressors: at his trial, on Calvary between two criminals, and in his death. That is the model for ministry—its vision and expectation—that the Lord puts upon the church: death and resurrection in service of the gospel to those around us.

8. Final summary

> Where the church and the mystery of the kingdom of heaven is, is not known except by the oral and public voice of the Gospel. . . . As the nets of the Apostles drew the fish in the water not toward the water but to the shore from the water . . . so Christ through the oral word draws Christians from things, places, and bodies, not into things, places, and bodies, in which by nature they already consist.[40]

Here Luther made one last appeal for the "oral and public voice of the Gospel." This is what makes ministers and pastors, professors and bishops: bearing the voice of God publicly to a world that wants nothing to do with God or that finds God boring, ineffectual, or dead. Christians get to shout from the rooftops that, in the words of J. B. Phillips, "We live on a visited planet"—visited by God himself in the manger and on the cross. This God continues the visit at baptism, washing the believer in the scarlet blood of Christ, at the Lord's Supper, where the believer feasts on Christ's body and blood in bread and wine, and in the believer's very ears every time someone stands up and proclaims God's forgiving mercy.

Luther's Response to Thomas Murner

Luther faced opposition to his theology and ecclesiology not just from the Italian papal party but also from the German one. At first, Jerome Emser, court theologian for Duke George of Saxony, that implacable opponent of Lutheranism, attacked Luther. The Wittenberger responded and provoked yet another salvo from Emser. Luther, who called Emser a goat because of that animal's presence on Emser's coat-of-arms, then wrote, "Answer to the Hyperchristian, Hyperspiritual, and Hyperlearned Book by Goat Emser in Leipzig—Including Some Thoughts regarding His Companion, the Fool Murner." As the title indicated, comments to Murner constituted a mere appendix.

Nevertheless, Murner's attacks on Luther are important, if for no other reason than that for the first time the charge was voiced that Luther's ecclesiology turned the church into a "Platonic republic," that is, an unreal, invisible institution. Luther puts it this way: "Since I had called the church a 'spiritual assembly,' you mocked me as though I wanted to build a church just as Plato built a city which is nowhere."[41] Luther's response is twofold. On the one hand, he insisted that the church is indeed spiritual and is not tied to particular places or people. He based his position, among other things, on the very texts he had used against Catharinus: God shows no partiality; you cannot say about the Kingdom of God, 'Lo, here it is.' He also used John 3— "That which is born of Spirit is spirit" and Stephen's comment in Acts 7 that God does not dwell in a temple made with hands.

For Luther, "fool Murner's" attack was anything but foolish. It struck at the very gospel Luther had rediscovered in Romans and now proclaimed to his flock in Wittenberg. Here as much as anywhere else Luther insisted on the spiritual nature of the church as an assembly of believers knit together in Christ. Justification *by faith alone* was not merely one quaint doctrine among many for Luther. On it, the church stands or falls—not merely in a doctrinal sense (that it must hold to justification) but in the very definition of the church itself!

On the other hand, Luther cited the creed ("I believe in . . . one holy Christian church") and argued that the church cannot be reduced to something one touches. If it could, then it would not require faith but would be simply a matter of sight. In this, the common, simple folk and children, who freely confess in the creed that they *believe* in the church, joined Luther against the papists. In later statements, some Lutherans would take back this point and search for a (visual) magisterial guarantee for the church's authority. Luther never did.

This second point may constitute the single greatest danger to contemporary ecclesiology: the presumption that we can "see" the church. The Nicene Creed is even clearer. The phrase, "We believe in one, holy, catholic, and apostolic church," far from defining the church's (visible) marks, calls for faith ("we *believe!*"), not sight. However, the next phrase, "We *acknowledge* one baptism for the forgiveness of sin," points instead to something physical and tangible: water and the word. In fact, the verbs in the creed demarcate an important shift (from believing to acknowledging) precisely at the point where the church's true *notae* first appear in the creed. "One, holy, catholic, and apostolic" are not the church's visible marks, baptism for the forgiveness of sins is. We simply cannot believe it!

This is the fatal flaw in present-day construals of ecumenical agreements. Christians assume that by entering into visible agreements they somehow can achieve church unity. This would be true *only* if we are not justified by faith alone without the works of the law. The Holy Spirit, working through God's word, has from the very beginning of the church been bringing about a far greater and more lasting unity, against which the gates of hell cannot prevail. Church unity, that is, our unity in baptism, Supper, and gospel, come as a gift from the Holy Spirit every time they occur.

Take, for example, how one may be tempted to interpret John 17:21, "That they may all be one." Countless times, well-meaning preachers use this text as a jumping-off point for the law. Their hearers are the ones who must guarantee, work at, and finally achieve church unity. However, Jesus—who generally understands things better than most preachers do in any case—is not praying to the disciples but to God the Father. Jesus realizes that unity comes not through our efforts but through the grace, mercy, and work of God. Moreover, this unity arises out of faith not out of institutions, because the line immediately before that famous text says, "I ask . . . on behalf of those who will believe in me through their word." The words immediately following the text describe not the unity of church structures but unity in God. "As you, Father, are in me and I am in you, may they also be in us, so that the world may believe that you have sent me." Following that, the text talks about the unifying nature of Christ's glory, not human glory ("The glory that you have given me I have given them, so that they may be one, as we are one"). True Christian unity is a given—what God achieves every time a child is baptized, a believer receives the Lord's Supper, or a preacher, of whatever stripe, proclaims the unconditional love and forgiveness of God in Christ. It is that unity, given through the word, which brings the world to faith that God sent Jesus and loves us (vv. 21, 23).

Conclusions

This chapter has moved from a mystery of history to the very heart of the gospel, all by asking about the characteristic markings of the church. What has this journey discovered along the way? First, Luther's ecclesiology is intimately connected to his proclamation of the gospel. Some of the difficulty experienced in the church today arises precisely because this connection has been broken. When the church ceases to be a creature of the word, it ends up undermining faith in God and resorting instead to human institutions and agreements as guarantees of the gospel. This, in turn, undermines the gospel of God's reconciliation in Christ and results in a peculiar form of works righteousness: salvation by right person and place.

Second, the marks of the church relieve Christians of the burden of creating or saving the church. Where the assembly hears the word and celebrates the sacraments, there God does church to them—that is, makes believers in the promise of Christ crucified and risen again. Here, Luther's ecclesiology comes as a breath of fresh air in the midst of the American addiction to methods and success. The life of the church does not depend upon its members but upon its Head. Or, as needs saying in most ordination sermons: someone has already died to save the church, so do not imagine you have to do it, too.

Third, the marks of the church—whatever the list—finally comes down to the gospel. It is the word alone! However, this crucial phrase can also easily turn into a slogan. For example, much of the present dissatisfaction with the ELCA and its ecumenical agreements has arisen *not* because of the word at all—despite the provocative web site bearing that name. Instead, it arises from the perception that some-one must guarantee the gospel but that the agreements chose the wrong someone. Certain voices among the "evangelical catholic" party may want that guarantee to come from apostolically successful bishops. Certain factions among the opponents to the recent agree-ment between the ELCA and the Episcopal Church, U.S.A., may want the guarantee to come from pastors, congregations, or even (in good American fashion) individuals. Either way, the gospel itself gets short-changed and leaves believers with no hope at all.

Despite the charges from Catharinus and Murner, Luther's ecclesi-ology is neither absurd nor abstract. It is also in no way incomplete.[42] Instead, it forces Christians to focus not on themselves but on God and God's word and to look for—to say nothing of ask, seek, and knock for—the characteristic markings, the signs of life in God, that comprise the church. This ecclesiology alone brings true concord and preserves the gospel. Moreover, as will become clear in a later chapter, this ecclesiology permeates every Lutheran confessional document and forms the perfect basis for understanding the public office of min-istry as service to the gospel alone.

Chapter 3

The Marks of the Church in the Liturgy

An Old Danish Picture of the Liturgy

One depiction of an assembly is the painting that was made by an anonymous artist in 1561 to hang on the front of the altar in the Torslunde parish church on Sjælland in Denmark (see p. 38). It hangs now in the Danish national museum in Copenhagen. It was made originally in order to set out, in a real community, a visual representation of what worship would be like if it followed the principles of the Reformation, a kind of measuring stick and reminder for the liturgical practice that would go on around that altar. The painting can be seen as one visual enacting of Luther's own discussion of the marks or signs by which someone may know "the Christian holy people." Even now, the painting says almost all that needs to be said about a Lutheran conception of church, about the Lutheran proposal in the ecumenical discussion of ecclesiology.

There is room for many different people in this image, as open as it is. They may come to word or bath or table, as if all these actions were happening together, interwoven with each other, leading to each other, interpreting each other. But as the people come, there is no fixed way of sitting or standing, no set way of dressing (even if you are clergy), and, we may infer, no established way of singing. The picture certainly shows a certain reception of tradition—say, in iconography or vestments. Why should these things be thrown out? The picture also shows a certain readiness for the new, the current, in clothing or in social patterns, and a refusal to compel one certain way of using those traditional matters that remain "indifferent." Mostly, however,

THE TORSLUNDE ALTAR PAINTING

the picture shows a great, open invitation and the powerful word, bath, table at the center. But even these central things, as diverse as they are, would fall apart except that they find their unity, like the unity of this otherwise fragmented picture, only in the cross of Christ. By the power of the Spirit, that death makes the communal use of the scripture to be the life-giving word of God, the communal taste of the meal to be the taste of the resurrection also for us now, the communal bathing with water to be a gathering of the flock by the good shepherd, a continual entry into this open assembly of witness to the needy world.

Here is a picture of assembly.

Of course, it is a picture from another time and place. It very likely does not look like "going to church," as many of us know it. But even with the differences—of clothing and postures and gender roles, to name a few—we can recognize the points of contact between assemblies we may know and this old one. We can recognize the marks of the church. Indeed, by seeing what we have in common with these

Christians of another time, we may see something profoundly true about assembly itself. We may see how this old assembly is still sending us the gift of its own central patterns, its own life in the Bible. And we may ask if these patterns have a future among us. Let the diverse groupings and postures of the people, the messiness of the picture, stand for the diversity of ways in which church may gather, sing, ritualize, engage in cultural communication, still today—especially today. Then, let preaching, baptism, and Holy Communion be what they are: the reasons we gather, in all of our diversities; the central matters for our gatherings, in sixteenth-century Denmark or in present-day North America. But these things, then and now, will be marks of the church when they are full of the word of the crucified one, the gospel that makes of bath, word, and table the acts of the living, life-giving God in our midst.

So how shall we find such an assembly?

Luther's List and the Augsburg Confession

That was Luther's question. His reflections on the signs or marks of the church certainly grew out of the polemics of the early sixteenth century, but they always had a pastoral turn, even in the midst of the fiercest controversy. How could a poor person, a needy person, find the assembly of God? How could you know it was there?

We have looked, with Timothy Wengert, at Luther's early use of this idea in response to the charge that he made of the church a Platonic reality not really available in the actual world. But the idea continues in the later work of Luther as well. The 1539 essay "On the Councils and the Church" was one preeminent place in which Luther sought to help "a poor confused person tell where such a Christian holy people are to be found in this world."[1] There he articulated seven tangible marks of the church, seven things you could see. Of course, elsewhere and in other context, the number and naming could be different. The list is not an inviolable system, an ecclesial metaphysics. It is rather the description of an event, of "church as a verb," as Timothy Wengert says. In the 1539 essay, these tangible matters of that event are summarized in this remarkable and memorable list:

- the preached word of God,
- the sacrament of Baptism,
- the Sacrament of the Altar,
- the use of absolution or the forgiveness of sins,
- the calling and consecrating of ministers,
- the public use of thanksgiving and prayer,
- and "the holy possession of the cross" (that is, the presence of suffering as a mark of the communal life).

Where one finds these signs, there "you may know that the church, or the holy Christian people, must surely be present."[2]

The Torslunde altar-front looks like a painting of this idea, a representation of church happening, a celebration that church has tangible signs. Preaching, baptism, and the sacrament of the altar are most obvious. But one must presume that public prayer has preceded and will follow these actions, especially the Holy Communion. And some people are praying now. Furthermore, ministers here are doing what ministers are called and consecrated for: serving the people with the gospel. Then, while no image of personal absolution is given, one may presume that the preaching, the baptizing, and the communing are indeed intended to proclaim the forgiveness of sins. And even though one does not see the suffering of this assembly, the very unity of the picture, the truth that draws all this motley lot into one, is the suffering of God as the welcoming and saving center for all the suffering of the assembly.

The Torslunde altar-front thus helps us see that Luther's marks of the church are at least to be understood as active liturgical realities. They are things that, by the mercy of God, actually go on in churches when people gather. The marks of the church should be taking place as the heart of any Christian assembly's liturgy. But even where they are only taking place in broken fragments, church is still beginning to happen.

For Luther, the signs and marks of the church inevitably go paired with liturgical assembly: the preached word "cannot be without God's people, and conversely, God's people cannot be without God's word."[3] The same thing can be said of baptism, Holy Communion, and the "keys" (the ministry of forgiveness): "wherever baptism and the sacrament are, God's people must be, and vice versa."[4] And since these things need communal participation and the leadership of a minister and server of the community in its use of word and sacrament, the same can even be said of ministry:

> Because he [sic] is in office and is tolerated by the assembly, you put up with him too. His person will make God's word and sacraments neither worse nor better for you. What he says or does is not his, but Christ, your Lord, and the Holy Spirit say and do everything, in so far as he adheres to correct doctrine and practice. . . . Now wherever you find these offices or officers, you may be assured that the holy Christian people are there; for the church cannot be without these bishops, pastors, preachers, priests; and conversely, they cannot be without the church. Both must be together.[5]

And the "holy possession of the cross" can at least come to expression liturgically. It will do that best not so much as a crucifix on the altar, but as prayer for the suffering, as collections of food and money for the wretched, as the confessed truth about our own need, and as an absence of triumphalism in worship. Indeed, such liturgical practice may well be despised by others as not positive enough and not tending toward "church-growth." When these things are present, together with the others, Luther might say, "you may know that the holy Christian church is there, as Christ says in Matthew 5, 'Blessed are you when men revile you and utter all kinds of evil against you on my account.'"[6]

What Luther is saying and what the Torslunde frontal is picturing sounds (and looks!) a great deal like the seventh article of the Augsburg Confession:

> It is also taught that at all times there must be and remain one holy, Christian church. It is the assembly of all believers among whom the gospel is purely preached and the holy sacraments are administered according to the gospel. For this is enough for the true unity of the Christian church that there the gospel is preached harmoniously according to a pure understanding and the sacraments are administered in conformity with the divine

Word. It is not necessary for the true unity of the Christian
church that uniform ceremonies, instituted by human beings,
be observed everywhere. As Paul says in Ephesians 4: "There is
one body and one Spirit, just as you were called to the one hope
of your calling, one Lord, one faith, one baptism."[7]

Note that evangelical preaching and the use of the sacraments are
not "ceremonies instituted by human beings" but the very central
signs of there being a church at all. Neither are we to imagine that we
can do without ceremonies. We should rather take this article of confession to mean that the great central signs of the church, which are
indeed truly universal by God's gift, will be enacted in each local
place and time in ceremonies that accord with the local reception of
history and with the gifts and dignity of each local culture. Such a
local region—even a region as large as, say, the churches in North
America—may certainly decide upon some local characteristics of
ceremonial commonality for the sake of mutual recognition and
order, as long as those decisions serve and do not obscure the centrality of the means of grace. Such decisions were taken in the sixteenth
century in the "church orders," *Kirchenordnungen* and *kyrkoordningen,* of
various Lutheran churches. And such decisions have been taken in
North America through such means as the *Use of the Means of Grace*
document[8] and the *Lutheran Book of Worship*[9] as well as other supple-
mentary worship materials. But it is not statements and printed liturgies that establish unity. From the point of view of the Augsburg
Confession, unity is given, rather, in that assembly around word and
sacrament for which statements and printed liturgies are intended as
resources and servants.

Set next to Luther's list and against the background of the biblical
understanding of "assembly," then, the text of the Augsburg Confession comes alive as a hermeneutical key. It can be seen as a profound
magna carta for the worship of the churches, a liturgical charter pointing both to the central things of any Christian assembly and to their
necessary localization. Indeed, there is a concrete, urgent, pastoral-
liturgical question resonating within the confession of this text: If the
preaching of the gospel and the celebration of the sacraments are central to the existence of church, are they actually seen as central, experi-

enced as central in our liturgies? But "Augustana VII" also establishes something else: the "method" of our realization of such a model of church—never by compulsion, by the legal enforcement of "universal ceremonies," but always by confession, preaching, teaching, example, encouragement, love.

A Danish Pastor and Teacher

This liturgical character of the confession about the church may become clearer to us by considering one other source of comment on the marks of the church: the work and influence of the nineteenth-century Danish scholar and hymn writer, bishop and theologian, Nicolai Frederik Severin Grundtvig.[10] The life of the churches and their mutual conversations could use some restoration of Grundtvig's work and influence. We will find that work to look a good deal like the Torslunde painting.

In much of his labor as a pastor, Grundtvig was seeking for the participation of the assembly in the central matters of church, central matters which he called "the Christian signs of life."[11] Such participation was found, for example, he argued, in the full communal engagement in that apostolic confession of faith made at the edge of the font and giving an enduring center to the church. So, he wrote in the mid-nineteenth century, "When I refer to the confession of faith at baptism of the ancient church I am referring to the audible 'Yes—Amen' of the congregation."[12] Grundtvig, too, was alive to the liturgical presence of the mystery of Christ at the heart of the participating congregation. With characteristic Lutheran accent, he called it "the living word." Indeed, for Grundtvig the test of the "word" is that it always says what baptism and the holy supper say to us:

> The fact that the Word from the mouth of the Lord is spoken to all of us at baptism and communion is the one true foundation for the faith of all Christians, old and young, wise and uninformed. This Word from the mouth of the Lord is the foundation for light and life; it is the rock and the sun, enlightening and enlivening in the Spirit of the Lord, which never deviates from what he has said.[13]

Indeed, for Grundtvig, the "word of God" was not first of all the Bible, certainly not the Bible as it was captive to the interpretations of various professors or held in a continually resurgent biblicism, but this "living word" of baptism and eucharist in which the meaning of the Bible was washed over the assembly and given to the assembly to eat and drink. With his remarkable skill for the memorable poetic word, Grundtvig himself crafted a hymnic phrase, which for anyone who knows Grundtvig, has stood as a sort of summary watchword for his insight, for what he called his "unparalleled discovery":

> Only at the bath and at the table,
> do we hear God's word to us.[14]

This is a summary watchword echoed in many of his hymns and elaborated in many of his sermons.[15] Indeed, if "God" here is taken to be the full presence of the life of the holy Trinity and if the assembly around "bath" and "table" is seen to include an opening toward all that is human, then this text can be seen to represent authentically the irreducible heart of Grundtvig's work. Even the "only" of the text can be seen as bringing to expression an important characteristic in the writings of Grundtvig: the polemical, classically Lutheran warmth with which he resisted both Protestant rationalist exegesis and biblicism as foundations for the church.

This accent on baptism and eucharist as the living word of God amid a participating, Sunday-gathering, "amen"-saying, singing, confessing congregation "produced its own kind of liturgical movement," observes Kenneth Stevenson, the current Anglican Bishop of Portsmouth,[16] "a popular sacramental awakening," writes Christian Thodberg, a Danish Lutheran pastor and theologian who now serves on the worship commission of the Danish church.[17] We may see Grundtvig's accent as marking the possibility that current Christians, under the influence of a fresh reading of the ancient church, of Luther, and of the Augsburg Confession, might turn their interest—in our time as in his—toward a recovered accent on sacramental presence, on congregational participation, and on social-critical cultural relevance.

Grundtvig, too, was uneasy with compulsion as a method for reform. Faced with the emergence of the conventicles of pietism in

Danish church life, he urged that the official "priesthood" of the Danish church and the officials of the state should refrain themselves from repression. The "marks of the church," the "Christian signs of life," are alive in his deeply Lutheran, Gamaliel-like counsel:

> No priesthood can therefore, no matter how genuinely apostolic it is, have a Christian basis for claiming a monopoly on preaching or on baptism. Priests may not claim dominion over the Christian light or over the Christian life. Under certain circumstances the reaction to alleged dominion may *breed* what we call "revivals or "godly assemblies," whose genuine Christianity nevertheless is not to be opposed by the priesthood as irresponsible lay efforts. They are to be judged in the same manner that the *priesthood* is judged, by their relation to the Christian confession, proclamation, and song of praise, and in an insoluble relation to baptism, which opens the Christian founts of life, and with Holy Communion, which creates and upholds the Christian stream of life in community with the Lord.[18]

So much is familiar to anyone who has read even a little of the prose or the hymns of Grundtvig as they are marked by his "churchly view" and who has thought about their presentation in the larger world. But what is much less well known is that the Grundtvig-influenced liturgical movement, the folk-based sacramental awakening, did have an American manifestation. While the small Grundtvigian Danish church in late nineteenth- and early twentieth-century North America was intensely creative—founding many folk-schools, for example, and adding its own new hymns and a vigorous new interest in world music to its Danish hymnic heritage—its contributions to American church-life were overshadowed and submerged, first in a bitter and church-dividing battle over the "Word of God"[19] and then in a continuing and nearly all-consuming concern about the nature of the preservation of Danish language and folk culture in its new setting. Nonetheless, the Danish American church did preserve for us a little text which is a treasure. It is a text worthy of the great Danish poet himself, setting the "marks of the church" into evangelical motion.

A Bell for the Liturgy

The text is found in one small settlement of Danish immigrants in northwestern Wisconsin, begun in 1869 in Polk County around Little Butternut Lake, and called West Denmark. Seven churches were ultimately built there, a folk-school briefly thrived, and, from 1887 to 1892, the first theological seminary of the Danish Evangelical Lutheran Church in America was housed in the folk-school building. One of the congregations of this community was (and is) called West Denmark Lutheran Church. In the steeple of the church building of that congregation there hung, until a tragic church fire in 1985, an inscribed bell, with the inscription speaking, in the manner of classic bell inscriptions, as if in the first-person of the bell. It is this inscription that concerns us:[20]

> Til badet og bordet,
> Till bønnen og ordet,
> Jeg kalder hver søgende sjæl.

> To the bath and the table,
> to the prayer and the word,
> I call every seeking soul.

Here is a text capable of being used as a summary of an abiding, ecumenical insight into the nature of "church" and an abiding contribution to liturgical renewal.

Indeed, unlike the famous "bath and table" hymn stanza, this bell inscription presents the Grundtvigian insight without polemics. Rather, the pastoral passion and existential address we know from Grundtvig the preacher speak here, inviting everyone to come to the great treasure of the living word.[21] The inscription is obviously Lutheran; it is an existential, pastoral reuse of the church definition of the Augsburg Confession. And it is that definition now turned toward invitation and the maintenance of an open door. The inscription can be used to summarize and rethink the meaning of the marks of the church.

The inscription itself is clear. "The bath and the table" are the central, church-defining actions to which people are invited. They are the gift and institution of Jesus Christ and the heart of Sunday assembly in the crucified and risen Christ. They are "means of grace," and "church" is there when these are the central actions. Participation in them will be participation in the mercy of the life-giving Trinity. Every Sunday assembly called together by this bell will be an encounter with this life-giving water—"creeping back to the font," Luther called it—and a celebration of the meal of this table. "The bath" is our introduction to this assembly, and we come past the bath—are in the reality of the bath again—whenever we are in the assembly. And "the table," occurring as the heart of the Sunday assembly, is the repeatable part of baptism. In such a way, the bell calls us to "church."

But then "the prayer" is also a gift of Jesus Christ and also a way in which humankind is held in the triune life of God, in God's very embrace.[22] "The prayer" is, most properly, the Lord's Prayer, that prayer given by Christ and, by the power of the Spirit in the assembly, full of Christ. The Lord's Prayer, of course, is always prayed as part of coming to the bath, prayed *at* the bath in that Lutheran liturgy of baptism which the Danish church inherited, prayed throughout the churches as part of the catechetical inheritance of the baptized. The Lord's Prayer gives us words for being in and of the bath. Furthermore, the Lord's Prayer gives us words for being at the table, at that place of the bread and forgiveness of God. It is always prayed, in all the churches, in the liturgy of the table. But then "the prayer" is also all prayer, understood in this same way as spoken in the power of the Spirit in and with Jesus Christ before the face of God. The Lord's Prayer, *the* prayer of the bath and the table, holds us in the life of the Triune God and forms us into intercessory prayer for all the needy world.[23] The prayer is both the presence and work of the Triune God and the ministry and work of the assembly.

"The word," then, is the very living word of God sounding throughout all of this assembly, in the grace-filled words of baptism, the supper, and the prayer: "I baptize you . . ."; "this is my body . . . my blood . . . given for you"; "give us this day the bread of the kingdom", "forgive us with your ultimate forgiveness now, even as we herewith forgive." "The word" is the biblical word come alive when bath, table, and prayer are seen as the hermeneutical key to the scriptures.

This was, of course, the very point at which the Danish church in North America faltered when faced with the fierce biblicism of the American frontier. It is a point on which the churches, faced with renascent biblicism, must not falter again. Rather, the bell echoes Grundtvig. Christian Thodberg writes:

> When for example Grundtvig preached on the story of the widow's son at Nain . . . he could maintain that Jesus' word to the widow, "Do not weep," and to the dead youth, "Rise up," cannot naturally relate to us; they were said to them then. Jesus' presence for us now is to be found in the words of the rite. "I declare," [says Grundtvig,] "just as surely as Jesus Christ is God's only begotten son, and just as surely as the baptism we are baptized with and the holy communion to which we are invited are instituted by him, so he is also present wherever people are baptized, are fed and nourished, on his behalf with his Word, and it is he himself who speaks to those who hear his voice. . . . Yes, this is my witness and therefore I have often said and I repeat that the Lord has met his people in the Spirit, as in today's Gospel he met the widow and her only son, has halted the bier and said to the church our mother, do not weep, and by awakening his Word from the dead through the means of grace he has awoken the church's hope and confidence which he in the end is himself, the Word of the living God."[24]

And Grundtvig echoes Luther: "When you open the book containing the gospels and read or hear how Christ comes here or there, or how someone is brought to him, you should therein perceive the sermon or the gospel through which he is coming to you, or you are being brought to him."[25] And Luther sounds like Ambrose. This conception of the role of the word in the assembly by no means involves the absence of scripture or preaching from the liturgy— witness Grundtvig's own preaching and the rich biblical imagery of his hymns!—but rather scripture seen as itself sacramental and liturgical preaching come alive. Indeed, such can be seen as the ancient church's sense of how scripture works in the assembly.

To all of these events on Sunday the bell invites *every seeking soul:* this is a meal for the hungry, as both Luther and Augustine would say. In fact, it is clear that the bell inscription envisions only "seeking souls" as potentially interested, invited ones here. All of us are seekers, in need of coming once again—and again—to faith. What happens in the assembly is addressed to seeking humanity, in touch with the actual realities of human life and the actual quests for meaning and for life that mark the depth of our days. The "house of the living word," by Grundtvig's conception, will echo with songs and actions that speak honestly of human experience, human life and death. This seeking character of our lives corresponds to what Lutherans regularly call "the law." The event of the assembly needs to take that law seriously and respond with what Lutherans call "the gospel." Then the very accessibility and existential importance of what occurs in the assembly is underscored the more by the words "bath" and "table," rather than more ecclesiastically appropriate words. The central events of the Sunday assembly are in critical but lively continuity with human experience and culture, with archetypal and recognizable human events like bathing and communal eating, just as were the meals of Jesus and the primitive Christian use of a great bath to mark the eschatological new beginning and the constitution of the eschatological community. The bell envisions that one comes through the door to a recognizable and attractive event: a real bath, a real meal, prayer before God, and in it all a word that matters for life.

Two other things, less clear, are also implied by the bell inscription. The first involves the role of *music:* just as the bell calls, musically, rhythmically, to bath, table, prayer and word, so also the music in the assembly itself is not some other, fifth thing. Rather, in the manner of the *Deutsche Messe* of Luther and the Danish *Højmesse* known by Grundtvig, music is the very mode in which the congregation gathers around and participates in the central matters of the assembly. It is not, ought not be, something else.[26]

The other matter is perhaps the most important. The bell remains rather mysterious as to *why* "every seeking soul" should come to the assembly. The content of the living word, the nature of bath, table, and prayer, the presence of the fullness of the gospel and the mercy of the Triune God are only known in the experience of the assembly itself, not in talking about the assembly nor in simply hearing the sound of the inviting bell. The actual, participating assembly—as long as it is indeed focused on bath and table, prayer and word—is the enacted *theologia prima* of the Christian church, as it encounters the crucified and risen one. There, experiencing this primary theology that engages our seeking, one understands why. It is as if the bell says, "Come and see." But then the "I" of the bell can be seen as something more, something mysterious as well. It is, of course, the bell itself, the actual ringing, inviting sound, so common in a Danish or an old Danish-American community. But it is also the Spirit of God, working on, in, and under all these human means, constantly reconstituting the church.

"To the bath and the table, to the prayer and the word, I call every seeking soul." This inscription offers a genuine insight into "church" in the present time, an insight capable of deepening and organizing our own efforts in the renewal of local assemblies of the church, our own actual *use* of the marks of the church. As we do so, there is one more text from Grundtvig that may help us. It is drawn from his 1863 essay, "Should the Lutheran Reformation Really Be Continued?"[27] Listen to him:

> When it happens that the priests stand at the baptismal bath as Zion's watchers in the power of the Spirit, and the bishop stands at the altar-table truly representing the Good Shepherd who lays down his life for the sheep, while the congregation gladly lets the light shine in good works, and the learned keep watch over the book with their lamps lit from the flame on the altar and keep watch that the church has open doors for going out as well as for coming in, then is everything in Christian order and then is the Lutheran Reformation complete.

Also for Grundtvig, ministry has its place in the assembly. Bishops help us first of all by their standing at the table, proclaiming and giving that word from which the church lives. But they also help us by encouraging the pastors to stand at the font and the learned to study the Bible in the light of the eucharist and to zealously guard the open door of the church.

Here is the important liturgical use of the marks of the church: Together we will need continually to see to it that our Sunday assemblies are actually centered in bath and table, prayer and word, accessibly present in the heart of participating communities. We will need to see to it that our buildings and our music, our leadership and our liturgies support this centrality and do not obscure it. We will need to encourage each other to continue to work on an existential, sacramental interpretation of scripture in the assembly, an interpretation that addresses all of our honest seeking with life-giving, grace-filled images. We need a word that bathes, a word that we can eat and drink and so live. We will need to work on a kind of participation that is lively—in singing, amen-saying, praying, bathing, eating and drinking, sending portions out through that open door—but still a participation that does not exclude. The participants are not insiders. All of us, including the ministers at the center of the circle, are seekers, beggars, in need of God. That will need to come to expression in our actual celebration. The theme will be: strong center, open door. Everyone should be welcome. All of our eucharists can be "seeker services." The idea of having separate, target-marketed, "seeker services" is such a bad idea. At the same time, we will need to reconstitute the way of the bath as a genuine and strong way—the catechumenal way—in which people can come more deeply into the purpose and life of the assembly.

Then we may be freed to see that "liturgy" always involves a diversity of cultural gifts—in diverse song and diverse texts, diverse human patterns of assembling and departing—gathered around the central things—word, bath, prayer, and table—as they are arranged in a meaningful order. Such a freedom will give us tools for authentic liturgical change. Grundtvig's accent on the central, enduring things of the assembly and his fierce interest in human culture and in the open door provide a rich theoretical basis for the constant inculturation of Christian liturgy. The liturgy, by this conception, is a focused pattern. Many cultural gifts may come into the assembly to gather around word, bath, and table, but not to make themselves the center of our gathering and the heart of our identity and our meaning. In that freedom, we may be newly and lovingly (if also critically) attentive ourselves to human culture and the deep human questions. The liturgical assembly is set in the midst of God's beloved world, and it requires honesty, not pretense or lies. And its door also opens *outward,* that we may flow into the life of the world, refreshed by a sense of the world as held in God's triune mercy.

So, let the marks be rung out at every open door: "To the bath and the table, to the prayer and the word, I call every seeking soul." And let them be enacted within. Then we need to inquire how we have, together, confessed these marks. But that is another chapter.

Chapter 4

The Marks of the Church in *The Book of Concord*

The Book of Concord contains documents best viewed in their historical and literary contexts. The point at which they apply most directly to the life of the church occurs precisely when one scrupulously maintains the vast historical differences between the Lutheran confessors and the present. At first glance, this assertion may seem self-evident. However, other approaches to these documents have often dominated during the past 475 years.[1] Orthodox Lutheran thinkers often inserted the confessions into larger theological systems or used them as answer books for later scholastic debates. Lutheran pietists, in fact (and not without some irony) accepted the judgment of the orthodox and sometimes denigrated the confessions as too rigid and doctrinal, favoring instead a recovery of the young Luther or a nondenominational approach to Christianity. Enlightened rationalists could sometimes reject them for much the same reason: they were far too particularistic for an age that was searching for the common denominator in all religions. Later, a romanticized view of the history could lead to the (false) assumption that the documents represented "the good old days," which one is called upon to repristinate in this age.

Viewed rigorously in context, however, these documents, like any good evangelical sermon, speak to the present in two ways. On the one hand, their alien character serves to judge our own hasty attempts at accommodation to this world or our sloppy attempts to worship the past. On the other, they sound a clarion call to the universal gospel of Jesus Christ. They preserve, so to speak, Christians caught in the act of confessing their faith. Thus, as Robert Kolb has argued, they preserve not only confessional documents or doctrine but the moment of confessing itself.[2] Thus, the *modus operandi* in this chapter will be quite simple. It will examine the Lutheran confessions carefully and demonstrate the crucial role that the marks of the church play in them. This will clarify the ways one can employ these documents to strengthen the witness of our church today.

The Augsburg Confession

At the heart of life together among Lutherans stands a single document, a confession of faith, called the Augsburg Confession. Using the ancient word for creed, *symbolon,* the Formula of Concord calls it "our symbol for this time," that is, equivalent to the creeds of the ancient church and consonant with them. One man, Philip Melanchthon, was responsible for most of the drafting of the text, although he used a bevy of prior documents in his work. Other theologians, chief among them the outlawed Martin Luther who could not accompany the Saxon entourage to Augsburg, approved it. A handful of princes, chief among them John, the elector of Saxony, and Philip, the landgrave of Hesse, and two imperial cities, including the powerful Nuremberg, subscribed it and presented it to the emperor, Charles V, on 25 June 1530. In our own day, some Lutherans view this document more as a theological straitjacket than (in accord with its original intention) as a confession of faith. The more the church can hear the strains of that original confessing voice, the more likely it can participate in the freedom of the gospel it offers.

The Structure of the Augsburg Confession
One must begin with some discussion of this document's form, in part because it is easy to misunderstand it completely by ignoring its actual structure.[3] Structure for Philip Melanchthon was never a matter of chance. In contrast, a student can sometimes read Luther's tracts and feel that when he wrote them he was setting off on a journey with no clear destination in mind (even though this, too, is rarely the case).

Especially for something as compact as this confession, Melanchthon used all of his skills as a writer and theologian to choose each word, each article, and even the order of each article with extreme care. Theologians and historians alike ignore his rhetorical and logical skills at their peril! Especially when examining the question of the marks of the church, one needs to keep this order in mind.

The Grand Division: Teaching and Practice
The first and most obvious division is between the first twenty-one articles and the last seven. In fact, in the original (now lost) documents, the *only* articles that received numbers were the last seven. The reasons for this are complex. Most important, the seven articles constituted the basis of the Saxon proposal for peace with the Roman church. Already before the presentation of the CA and certainly afterwards, both Melanchthon and Luther, as well as the Saxon court, insisted that all they sought from Rome was permission to change a few practices. In exchange, they would again accept the authority of the bishops in communion with Rome. The list varied but always included married priests, communion in both kinds, and a single Sunday mass (instead of the private sacrificial masses said daily at many churches). These three constitute articles XXII–XXIV. Confession, foods, and monastic vows (articles XXV–XXVII) were less important but also described obvious changes in practice in evangelical territories. CA XXVIII then pointed a way to define the episcopate in an evangelical manner and to overcome division in the church.[4]

The first twenty-one articles, by contrast, contained a brief evangelical exposition of the Christian faith. Based in general on a creedal order, this section represented a thorough reworking of an earlier document, the Schwabach Articles. Those articles, written in the summer of 1529, had been the official confession of faith for Electoral Saxony. The statements in these twenty-one articles were, to use modern parlance, nonnegotiable, because to the reformers they simply reflected the faith of the church of all ages. To abandon these articles would be to abandon the gospel itself and to betray Christ. The currently popular notion of reading the CA backwards, from article

XXVIII, downplays the centrality of the first section.[5] The evangelical party at Augsburg in general and Philip Melanchthon in particular actually thought this first section reflected the church's faith and that their confession would achieve widespread acceptance. Despite rejection by Roman theologians at Augsburg, the CA indeed did just that, as more and more cities, principalities, and theologians subscribed to it in the coming years. Even today, for example, these articles have shaped the historic confessions of faith for every ecumenical partner with which the ELCA has recently forged agreements. Regarding the marks of the church, the Augsburg Confession discusses them in both sections and to very different ends. In the first, they arise in discussions of ministry and church (CA V and VII). In the second, they define the office of bishop.

The Shape of CA I–XXI
A detailed examination of the first part of the Augsburg Confession reveals how carefully Melanchthon structured this section. First, as already mentioned, one can discern a creedal organization. No wonder it refers to the ancient creeds twice (in CA I and III). CA I deals with the person and nature of God (topics associated with the First Article of the creed). CA II–III examine sin and redemption (that is, the Second Article of the creed). CA IV–XVII describe the work of the Holy Spirit through the word in saving us and making us holy in the church (the Third Article).[6] Articles XVIII–XXI are more or less appendices, added by Melanchthon in Augsburg to deal with specific issues in dispute. CA XVIII and XIX touch on questions that arose in the debate between Luther and Erasmus on free will and reflect precisely Melanchthon's own refutation of Erasmus in this dispute.[7] CA XX and XXI answer charges by John Eck and actually handle practical issues (preaching and prayer) that, unlike CA XXII–XXVIII, are not matters for debate but go to the very heart of the gospel and divine worship.[8]

Within the creedal, or Trinitarian, shape of the doctrinal articles of the CA, Melanchthon interwove certain substructures. Thus, without mentioning creation directly in CA I, he implied as much in CA II. Similarly, CA IV marks a transition between the second and third articles of the creed. Each of the first nineteen articles has more or less the same shape. Melanchthon introduced each statement of evangelical teaching with "It is taught" or "they [the princes' teachers] teach." After stating the doctrine ("concerning x"), he often supplied Bible verses or statements of the church fathers or creeds to prove the point. Many articles end with a list of condemnations, imitating pronouncements of the Council of Nicea and other ecumenical councils.

The original twenty-one articles were probably not numbered and certainly not given titles, which first appeared in the seventeenth century. In fact, the first heading comes with article twenty (in the German), "concerning faith and good works." It would seem that the *Confutatio,* that refutation of the CA presented in Augsburg by Roman theologians in August 1530, numbered the first twenty-one articles. Unfortunately, this numbering, whenever it occurred, had the effect of disintegrating the original unity of the document and turning it into a set of theological loci rather than a confession of faith. Still later, titles for the articles did the same thing.

By eliminating the numbering and titles and instead concentrating on the shape of the articles, one discovers that in two crucial instances numbering and labeling the articles have separated articles that originally belonged together. Both CA V and CA VIII lack the standard introduction ("concerning x" or "it is taught"). Instead, they flow directly from the preceding articles. Moreover, the preceding articles (CA IV and VII) lack condemnations that instead come at the end of the articles that follow. Thus, there is an intimate, literary connection between CA IV and V and between CA VII and VIII. Interestingly enough both contain references to the marks of the church.

Before leaving the question of structure, it is necessary to observe how Melanchthon organized articles IV–XVII. One question that often arose for Melanchthon was where to place the sacraments: under the church or under the gospel. He experimented with various approaches in his theological textbooks. However, in the CA, perhaps reflecting the creedal order (where mention of the church precedes Holy Baptism and the forgiveness of sin), he separated the sacraments (articles IX–XIII) from the gospel (articles IV–VI). As it stands, the CA has this order: Work of the Holy Spirit (CA IV–VI:

gospel, ministry, and good works), Church (CA VII–VIII), Sacraments (CA IX–III), Ecclesial Order (CA XIV–V), Social Order (CA XVI), and Eschatology (CA XVII). By placing the sacraments after the church, Melanchthon could then distinguish between required church practices (the sacraments and call, CA IX-XIV) and human traditions (CA XV), before turning in CA XVI to a completely new topic, governmental order.

The Marks of the Church in CA V–VI and VII–VIII, XV

> Furthermore, it is taught that we cannot obtain forgiveness of sin and righteousness before God through our merit, work, or satisfactions, but that we receive forgiveness of sin and become righteous before God out of grace for Christ's sake when we believe that Christ has suffered for us and that for his sake our sin is forgiven and righteousness and eternal life are given to us. For God will regard and reckon this faith as righteousness in his sight, as St. Paul says in Romans 3 and 4. To obtain such faith God instituted the office of preaching, giving the gospel and the sacraments. Through these, as through means, he gives the Holy Spirit who produces faith, where and when he will, in those who hear the gospel. It teaches that we have a gracious God, not through our merit but through Christ's merit, when we so believe. Condemned are the Anabaptists and others who teach that we obtain the Holy Spirit without the external word of the gospel through our own preparation, thoughts, and works.[9] (CA IV–V)

The chapter on the origins of the marks of the church indicated that for Luther the word of God (not simply in a book or flowery speech, but in true Christian proclamation of the gospel) was the central sign and identifying characteristic of the church. In CA IV–V, Melanchthon said much the same thing. At the same time, he anticipated another trenchant evangelical insight: The marks of the church occur when the Holy Spirit delivers the Word and sacraments through the public office of ministry.

In the way he linked articles IV and V, Melanchthon underscored the centrality of the Word of the gospel. CA IV begins, "Further-

more, it is taught that we cannot obtain forgiveness of sin and righteousness before God through our merit . . . but that we receive forgiveness of sin and become righteous before God out of grace for
Christ's sake through faith when we believe that Christ has suffered
for us. . . ." It then refers to Romans 3 and 4, the first biblical references in the CA. However, Melanchthon immediately added: "To
obtain such faith, God instituted the office of preaching, giving the
gospel and the sacraments." Thus, Melanchthon bound justification
and the preaching office together. To be sure, CA V does not understand this office clericalistically. Nevertheless, Melanchthon was not
referring to the priesthood of all believers. The term *Predigtamt* (literally, "preaching office," but often used more generally for "pastoral
office") precludes that.[10]

At the same time, Melanchthon made clear that this office of
preaching is transparent. It is not about specific guarantors or specific
places but about the gospel and sacraments. It is not so much *who*
does these things but *whether* they are done at all. In an emergency,
any Christian must step in and fill the office of preaching. Thus,
authority rests not in the officeholder but in the Holy Spirit, who uses
these means of grace to work faith "where and when he pleases." This
will become clearer in the chapter on the older Luther.

Why emphasize the external word to such a degree? For one thing,
this concern matched Luther's earliest comments on the church. For
another, it allowed Melanchthon to contrast evangelical teaching to
Anabaptists and others who, to quote CA V, "teach that we obtain the
Holy Spirit without the external word of the gospel through our own
preparation, thoughts, and works." The Latin is even clearer. "[They]
think that the Holy Spirit comes to human beings without the external Word through their own preparations and works." Who were
these "other people"? As a note in the present translation indicates,
these were the evangelicals' own opponents in Augsburg. Following
their favorite teacher, Gabriel Biel, these people taught that, quite
apart from the word of the gospel and simply by exercising their own
natural powers, God gives grace to "those who do what is in them."[11]

What, then, do these two articles say about the marks of the church?
The gospel is central. This gospel is specifically the forgiveness of sins

and righteousness obtained by Christ and bestowed by the Holy
Spirit through the proclaimed word and sacraments. As Matt. 10:27
puts it, this word demands to have a public voice. "What you hear
whispered, proclaim from the housetops!" The authority of this
office (as opposed to the authority to fill the office) does not come
from the church but arises directly from the word itself and the Holy
Spirit. Moreover, this office has no independent authority but is
completely transparent. It fulfills its office when it delivers the goods
not when it claims to have authority. As Gerhard Forde has described
it,[12] the office of ministry is like the office of letter carrier. The letter
carrier, like the pastor, fulfills his or her office only when delivering
the mail.

Finally, both the marks of the church and this public office—by
virtue of the very Word of forgiveness in Christ—stand in stark contrast to those who imagine that human beings reach God by "their
own preparations and works." Thus, CA IV–V, by their literary connection, demonstrate again that the marks of the church, far from
being peripheral to Lutheran theology, arise from the very center of it,
from justification by faith alone.

> It is also taught that at all times there must be and remain one
> holy, Christian church. It is the assembly of all believers among
> whom the gospel is purely preached and the holy sacraments are
> administered according to the gospel. For this is enough for the
> true unity of the Christian church that there the gospel is
> preached harmoniously according to a pure understanding and
> the sacraments are administered in conformity with the divine
> Word. It is not necessary for the true unity of the Christian
> church that uniform ceremonies, instituted by human beings,
> be observed everywhere. As Paul says in Ephesians 4[:4-5]:
> "There is one body and one Spirit, just as you were called to the
> one hope of your calling, one Lord, one faith, one baptism."
> Likewise, although the Christian church is, properly speaking,
> nothing else than the assembly of all believers and saints, yet
> because in this life many false Christians, hypocrites, and even
> public sinners remain among the righteous, the sacraments—
> even though administered by unrighteous priests—are effica-
> cious all the same. For as Christ himself indicates [Matt.

23:2-3]: "The scribes and the Pharisees sit on Moses' seat. . . ." Condemned, therefore, are the Donatists and all others who hold a different view.[13]

Concerning church regulations made by human beings, it is taught to keep those that may be kept without sin and that serve to maintain peace and good order in the church, such as specific celebrations, festivals, etc. However, people are also instructed not to burden consciences with them as if such things were necessary for salvation. Moreover, it is taught that all rules and traditions made by human beings for the purpose of appeasing God and of earning grace are contrary to the gospel and the teaching concerning faith in Christ. That is why monastic vows and other traditions concerning distinctions of foods, days, and the like, through which people imagine they can earn grace and make satisfaction for sin, are good for nothing and contrary to the gospel.[14] (CA VII-VIII, XV)

How many times have theologians, historians, bishops, and pastors in the ELCA during the last few years debated the significance of CA VII?[15] Does the phrase "It is enough" imply that one ought not enter into full communion with the Episcopal Church, U.S.A., a church that insists upon the historical succession of bishops for full communion with another church? One path through those arguments over *satis est* ("it is enough"), without rehearsing the entire debate, may open up by examining the actual words and structure of the entire article of the church (CA VII, VIII, and [!] XV). Perhaps this will shed a little light on this heated topic.

First, the article headings are confusing. CA VII and VIII together provide a definition of the church. They represent not, as some often complain, an incomplete ecclesiology but, in the words of John Ehrlichman, "the whole enchilada." What is missing, as will be shown, is precisely the kinds of guarantors that the gospel itself eliminates but that many Christian theologians seem incapable of living without.

Second, right out of the gate Melanchthon defined church in such a way as to eliminate all searching after the proper "person" or "place" for the church. He did this in two strokes. On the one hand, he began by talking about the eternal nature of the church. Here, the German reflects the language of the creed: "It is also taught that at all times there must be and remain one holy, Christian church." Such a beginning was quite unusual for Melanchthon and his Aristotelian method. When in his work on dialectics Melanchthon summarized Aristotelian logic, he defined a series of questions that thinkers may address to each topic. These included whether a thing exists, what it is, what its parts are, what it is similar to or different from, what its causes are, what its effects are. For Wittenberg's foremost dialectician, the crucial questions were what a thing is and what its effects are. In CA VII, however, he actually began with Aristotle's first question: not so much whether a thing exists as how long it will exist, which amounts to the same thing.

By insisting on its eternality, Melanchthon forced Lutherans to be ecumenical, in the full sense of the term. They cannot, like the Jehovah's Witnesses, Mormons, or other offspring of the American religious experience, imagine a time on earth when the church did not exist. Both Luther and Melanchthon consistently traced the origins and continuity of the church not simply from Jesus and the apostles but from the Garden of Eden itself. Moreover, the 1400 years of the church's history between the last apostle and the Lutheran Reformation were not blank pages. Melanchthon also insisted, however, that whatever the church was, it transcended time, place and person. Whatever "church" is in CA VII–VIII, it is *not* some separate, pure Lutheran denomination per se or any other social or political entity. Human beings, whether believers or not, are not the subject of the verb in these articles.

To sever the ties between particular places and persons and the church, Melanchthon also, on the other hand, defined the church as "the assembly of all believers" ("saints" in the Latin). This, too, not only eliminates the Lutheran church or the church of Rome or some pious Lutheran congregation in, say, Roberts, Wisconsin, as sole proprietors or guarantors of church, but it also has significant ecumenical implications. Wherever one finds an assembly of believers and saints—their faith and holiness having been defined in CA IV–VI— there is church. This meant that in the sixteenth century, Lutherans had an immediate openness to the Eastern Orthodox churches, to the Hussites, and even to their Roman opponents. Lutherans could never legitimately say, outside of the *Lutheran* church or the church in Wittenberg there is no salvation.

Of course, as Luther experienced from the start, opponents will ask, "But where is such a church?" Defining the church in terms other than place or person forced Melanchthon immediately to invoke the marks of the church. Note the subtle difference between the German and Latin. The German refers back to the people and says, "among whom," while the Latin refers back to the assembly and church and states, "in which." The "among" harks back to Jesus' line, cited by Luther, "The kingdom of God is among you." The "in" here does not define the church by a place but instead a place by the church. That is, it is not, "We have the church in this place, therefore we must have word and sacrament," but "Here are word and sacrament, therefore we are in church."

Now the words "purely preached" and "administered according to the gospel" become crucial for the discussion. The second phrase (simply "rightly administered" in the Latin) is the easiest to understand. This is not some magical, imprecise phrase—the last, best threat of orthodox seminary professors to their students departing for the parish ("Do it right, or else!"). Instead, it refers precisely to what the second half of the document, in CA XXII and XXIV, claim: communion in both kinds and a Lord's Supper celebrated without sacrifice. It also refers to articles IX–XIV, which define the sacraments in detail.

Once that becomes clear, one can more easily determine what pure preaching and teaching of the gospel mean. The reformers had in mind precisely what is in the first twenty-one articles of the CA. This is *not* because they are so enamored of their own theological opinions, but because they actually do believe and are confessing that these articles reflect the pure gospel. In particular, Melanchthon was referring here to CA I–VI: God, Original Sin, Christ, Justification (including good works), but especially to CA IV–VI. Melanchthon expressly indicated this in CA XX, where he had opportunity to define the gospel for a second time in the document.

> Our people have taught as follows: In the first place, our works cannot reconcile us with God or obtain grace. Instead this happens through faith alone when a person believes that our sins are

forgiven for Christ's sake, who alone is the mediator to reconcile the Father. . . . We must also explain that we are not talking here about the faith possessed by the devil and the ungodly, who also believe the story that Christ suffered and was raised from the dead. But we are talking about true faith, which believes that we obtain grace and forgiveness of sin through Christ. . . . Further, it is taught that good works should and must be done, not that a person relies on them to earn grace, but for God's sake and to God's praise. Faith alone always takes hold of grace and forgiveness of sin. Because the Holy Spirit is given through faith, the heart is also moved to do good works.[16]

In CA VII.1 Melanchthon defined the heart of Lutheran ecclesiology: the church lasts forever and is an assembly of believers, marked by Word and Sacrament. Only then did he turn to two questions: the nature of Christian unity (CA VII.2–4) and the role of human purity in the church (CA VIII). As far as unity went, all that mattered was harmony and agreement in word and sacrament. This has far-reaching consequences, because here Melanchthon had enshrined Luther's insights from his debate with Catharinus. First, the marks of the church are the basis of Christian unity. Second, it means that everything else is secondary and a matter of *indifferentia* (a term that does not, however, mean *inconsequentia*). Third, the scriptural passage that sets the Lutheran ecumenical table is Ephesians 4: "one body, one Spirit, one hope, one Lord, one faith, one baptism, one God and Father of us all." That is, Christians receive unity in the Triune God (Spirit, Lord, Father), in our faith and hope, in baptism, and thus in the one body of the church. This is nothing short of unity in word (professing the Trinity, hope, and faith) and sacrament (here represented by baptism).

At the same time, two things were *not* necessary for church unity. The first is uniformity in ceremonies instituted by human beings. Melanchthon explained this topic more fully in CA XV, to which we must now turn. After defining the sacraments, where there must be unity (CA IX–XIII), Melanchthon returned to the question of human traditions and regulations in the church (CA XIV–XV). In today's church this might include, among other things, the tradition of apostolic succession (something Anglicans invoked especially beginning in the nineteenth century) or congregational autonomy (something beloved by certain strains of nineteenth-century American Lutheran pietism). All such regulations fall under the first use of the law in the church, where the law maintains order and restrains evil. In the world, God maintains this order through government, as CA XVI describes. In the church, Melanchthon wrote in CA XV, ecclesial regulations maintain peace and good order.

Melanchthon also limited such regulations in two ways. First, they dare never be confused with salvation and thus become a burden for consciences. (This also relates to the discussion in the Epitome below.) Second, no one can confuse them with the gospel and champion their fulfillment as a means of earning God's grace. Only if they cross either of these two lines can a Lutheran object substantively to regulations. Of course, we can argue whether to sing Advent hymns during Christmas or whether to include Presbyterians when installing Lutheran bishops, but never on substantive grounds—only on the grounds of what best serves the church. Compared with the gospel, all these things are *indifferentia*.

The other thing not necessary for church unity is ministerial or congregational purity. This comprises the single greatest temptation among American Christians. The heresy is Donatism—the insistence that only holy people may deliver to God's people holy things. This heresy was a plague in North Africa at the time of Augustine. A split had occurred in the church because some had alleged that among the bishops at the consecration of the bishop of Carthage were some who had been *traditores* (literally: people who hand over), from which we get our word traitor. That is, they had handed over sacred books to the pagan authorities during persecution. Consequently, this party established its own bishops and refused to recognize catholic bishops as true bishops.

Part of Augustine's answer to this group was to argue that the sacraments of the church belonged to God not to the officiants, and that no sin of theirs could block God's grace to the believer. In the seventeenth century, a variation on the Donatist heresy arose in England and was transported soon thereafter to New England. Adherents bore the name Puritan, in part because moral purity had become the watchword for the true church. It is interesting to note that these groups also have a very low tolerance for adiaphora. This puritanical view came to dominate American church life. It is epitomized in the telephone call I received from an intern six or seven years ago. She recounted how her supervisor had run off with the church secretary and how subsequently members of her congregation had asked her whether they needed to have their babies rebaptized.

Returning to article VIII, Melanchthon had two motives for including this article here. First, he wanted to answer the objection of some of his opponents who, when they heard that the church was the gathering of saints and believers, immediately accused him of Donatism. Second and more important, he wanted to distance the evangelical party at Augsburg from people like Ulrich Zwingli and others, who broke from the church on moral grounds. Luther was always proud of saying that there were worse sinners in Wittenberg than in Rome. Moral goodness does not define the church; only the word and sacraments do. However, this resulted in Melanchthon inadvertently providing yet other grounds for Lutheran ecumenism. This article implies that Lutherans cannot reject the sacraments of other churches out of hand. There is never any thought of rebaptizing Roman Catholics or Anabaptists or Zwinglians for that matter. A pastor's bad theology or morals cannot invalidate his or her baptizing, celebrating the Supper, or (according to the Latin) even preaching.

What freedom this implies for the preachers themselves! How often have I preached when filled with doubts and uncertainties! How often have I sinned in midst of celebrating the Lord's Supper! But, as Luther was fond of saying, God is bigger than our doubts, bigger than our sins. Or, as Melanchthon put it succinctly in the Latin version of CA VIII, "Both the sacraments and the Word are efficacious because of the ordinance and command of Christ, even when offered by evil people." That comes as no small relief to most pastors and bishops.

The Marks of the Church in CA XXVIII

CA XXVIII is too long to cite in its entirety here. Nevertheless, it forms a crucial part of the discussion. Here especially, however, one must untangle the complexities of sixteenth-century life and thought.[17] First, the bishops of Germany were also territorial lords. Thus, some people would look to the bishop as secular prince as well as ecclesiastical prelate, others only as prelate. Second, some powerful imperial cities that were also episcopal sees had begun already in the fifteenth century the process of eliminating the bishop's political control so that they could be completely independent of his rule. This was, for example, the case in Nuremberg, an original signer of the Augsburg Confession, where they wanted nothing to do with bishops at all. It is all the more remarkable that they signed the document, given its generally positive statements about bishops. Third, the reformers themselves had in the course of the Reformation rediscovered that in the early church and even in the Pastoral Epistles of 1 Timothy and Titus, bishops were simply the chief pastors in a particular town. Thus, in his correspondence, Luther will sometimes address such a chief pastor as bishop. He often referred to Wittenberg's chief pastor, Bugenhagen, as bishop. There were other pastors in Wittenberg, including Luther, but only Bugenhagen was called bishop. This means, by the way, that already at the outset of the Lutheran Reformation, there was never any attempt to eliminate bishops or to champion what some call a "presbyteral succession," let alone congregational autonomy. Lutherans have always assumed that there is structure and governance in the church beyond the local congregation. Thus, whenever it became politically impossible to use the term "bishop," they called such people "superintendents," a Latin rendering of the Greek ἐπίσκοπος. Likewise, when the first evangelical bishops came to power, they were accorded the exclusive right to ordain in their diocese.[18] All of these competing notions about bishops were playing themselves out in CA XXVIII, with the result that modern readers often cannot understand what Melanchthon was trying to say.

Rather than try to sort out all of these strands, this section will highlight two of the more important ones. First, the title, which was original to the document, tells us that the issue here is not so much the nature of bishops but their power ("Concerning the Power of the Bishops"). The Latin ("Concerning the Church's Power"), in referring to the church, more accurately depicts the fact that true power in the church rests not in any office but with the church itself. Of course, to quote St. Paul, God makes this power perfect in weakness, an insight dealt with in the chapter on the old Luther.

Second, the document immediately recognizes that mixing governmental authority with the authority of bishops was a mistake. "Some have improperly mixed the power of bishops with the secular sword, and such careless mixture has caused many extensive wars, uprisings, and rebellions." Even today, with the bishop of Rome controlling the Vatican and Roman Catholic bishops suggesting that sensitive documents be sent to the Vatican's American embassy for protection, the same confusion still reigns. When the pope accepts a Christmas tree from an Austrian state governor who has neo-Nazi leanings, it is not simply a mistake or an exercise in Christian tolerance but instead a political act. No wonder the Italians were up in arms! One can scarcely imagine what that kind of mixture meant during the Reformation. The closest Americans have to such a mix occurs when a cleric, such as Jesse Jackson or Pat Robertson, runs for president. But even these men were running for president not as pastors but as citizens.

For Melanchthon, at the heart of the problem was a failure to recognize the characteristic markings of the church and, hence, the office of ministry and to distinguish that office from the government. Melanchthon put it this way:

> Our people teach as follows. According to the gospel, the power of the keys or of the bishops is a power and command of God to preach the gospel, to forgive or retain sin, and to administer and distribute the sacraments. . . . Not bodily but eternal things and benefits are given in this way, such as eternal righteousness, the Holy Spirit, and eternal life. These benefits cannot be obtained except through the office of preaching and through the administration of the holy sacraments. . . . Now inasmuch as the power of the church or of the bishops bestows eternal benefits and is used and exercised only through the office of preaching, it does not interfere at all with public order and secular authority. For secular authority deals with matters altogether different

from the gospel. Secular power does not protect the soul but, using the sword and physical penalties, it protects the body and goods against external violence.[19]

Here, forgiveness of sin (CA IV), the office of preaching (CA V), the nature of the church (CA VII–VIII), and the marks of the church coalesce. The characteristic markings of the church are unlike the markings of government and thus serve very different purposes. Even today, the confusion of these two hands of God can cause immeasurable harm to the gospel of Jesus Christ and his church. The authority of bishops and the office of preaching and administering the sacraments converge in the marks of the church. Anything else a pastor or bishop does is not gospel, has nothing to do with the marks of the church, and dare not be confused with the pastoral calling. The reason there is in the Lutheran tradition no difference between *presbyteros* (pastor) and *episkopos* (bishop) lies in a single fact: what they do is the same. The question of authority remains secondary to the gospel. Whether one preaches to an entire synod or to an individual congregation, the authority and office remain the same: delivering the good news of God in Christ reconciling the world into God's very heart.

CA XXVIII also tells the reader very clearly what a bishop's divine, God-given calling is.

> Consequently, according to divine right it is the office of the bishop to preach the gospel, to forgive sin, to judge doctrine and reject doctrine that is contrary to the gospel, and to exclude from the Christian community the ungodly whose ungodly life is manifest—not with human power but with God's Word alone. . . . Whatever other power and jurisdiction bishops have in various matters . . . they have them by virtue of human right.[20]

Here again the marks of the church crop up. Every pastor has this authority. When he or she stands in the pulpit, baptizes or presides at the table, opens the mail, leads a council meeting, presides at a synod assembly, or teaches at a seminary, the responsibility is the same: get the gospel out by forgiving sins. What follows—discerning good teaching from bad and godly behavior from ungodly—is not an arbitrary right detached from the gospel but arises precisely from the gospel itself. The only reason Christians need to foster pure teaching and restrain ungodliness is for the little ones in their care. Taken in themselves, bad teaching and perverse public behavior do not hurt anyone but the ones doing them. However, such things do not simply occur in a vacuum; they always reach out and shake the faith of others, of the weak and uncertain ones.

For the sake of the weak, pastors must worry about what they teach and preach and how they behave. Every pastor and bishop knows that misconduct by a member of the clergy, once it comes to light, affects everyone in a congregation, synod, and church. Recent sexual scandals among the Roman Catholic clergy have affected all clergy everywhere. However, does anyone realize what happens when a bad sermon comes spewing forth from a preacher's lips? The judging of bad doctrine is not simply a matter of groaning every time some benighted church bureaucrat writes something unforgivable in a church document. It happens on a weekly basis in many congregations, synods, and seminaries. Yet how loath we are to intervene! If it were only a matter of power politics and human relations, we could well refrain from getting mixed up in anything so personal. But every week simple, trusting souls return home unfed—having never heard the good news of forgiveness through Christ's death and the consolation of eternal life through his resurrection. If thousands throng to the church-growth meccas of the world but never hear the gospel, then they have not gone to church. In fact, there may be fewer people in such a gathering than in a meeting of forty huddled around the gospel and sacraments in a clapboard church on the wind-swept prairies of Nebraska. What matters are always the markings, the feathers, of this bird called the church. The public office of ministry is to prevent the wholesale plucking of it.

Other Documents Written by Philip Melanchthon

The scope of these essays does not permit as thoroughgoing an investigation of the other documents in *The Book of Concord*. However, each

of the other documents contributes to an understanding of the marks
of the church and their function in the Reformation.

The Apology of the Augsburg Confession

There is a single passage in Ap VII/VIII that illustrates the remarkable
convergence in Melanchthon and Luther's understanding of the marks
of the church. It also demonstrates that Melanchthon was intimately
aware of the origins of this teaching, referring indirectly to the early
attack of Thomas Murner mentioned above. Melanchthon wrote:

> Nor indeed are we dreaming about some platonic republic, as
> some have slanderously alleged. Instead, we teach that this
> church truly exists, consisting of true believing and righteous
> people scattered through the entire world. And we add its marks
> [*notae*]: the pure teaching of the gospel and the sacraments.[21]

Here Melanchthon had supplied, for the first time in an official document of the evangelical churches, the soon-to-become technical term,
notae. Moreover, he already pledged evangelical teachers to an ecumenical understanding of church, the unity of which rests not in a
place or person but in the work of the Holy Spirit through the word.
The church consists of believers scattered throughout the world
marked by word and sacraments.

Later in the same article, Melanchthon took up another challenge
from the Confutation, the Roman party's response to the CA, in
which they had rejected the CA's claim that the gospel and sacraments were enough for unity by stating that there must also be unity
in universal rites. Melanchthon's language made it abundantly clear
he was not talking about church mergers or ecumenical agreements
but precisely about what happens when the Holy Spirit unites us in
faith around the word—spoken and visible. He wrote:

> We do not quite understand what the opponents want. We are
> speaking about a true unity, that is, a spiritual unity, without
> which there can be no faith in the heart nor righteousness in the
> heart before God. For this unity we say that it is not necessary
> to have similar human rites, whether universal or particular,
> because the righteousness of faith is not a righteousness tied to

certain traditions, as the righteousness of the law was tied to Mosaic ceremonies. For this righteousness of the heart is a matter that makes the heart alive. Human traditions, whether universal or particular, contribute nothing to this giving of life. Nor are they caused by the Holy Spirit, as are chastity, patience, the fear of God, love of one's neighbor, and works of love.[22]

For Melanchthon, everything else was secondary to the gospel. That is the ground of true Christian unity—something the Holy Spirit has been working and will continue to work in the saints through the Word from the beginning of the world to the end.

The Treatise on the Power and Primacy of the Pope

In addition to the Treatise's refutation of the notion that the pope had some sort of God-given authority in the church, Melanchthon also revisited the question of episcopal authority. In general, he simply referred readers back to the CA and Ap. In the Treatise, the marks of the church are front and center for defining ministry. "The gospel bestows upon those who preside over the church the commission to proclaim the gospel, forgive sins, and administer the sacraments." What could be simpler than that? And to think that pastors get paid to participate in these treasures of the church! Melanchthon subjoined, "In addition, [the gospel] bestows the legal authority, that is, the charge to excommunicate those whose crimes are public knowledge and to absolve those who repent."[23] Here, Melanchthon maintained the differentiation between the gospel and protection of the weak, pointed out above in the discussion of CA XXVIII. His basic argument here, however, centered in the equality of presbyters and bishops. Because the church in Wittenberg had started ordaining pastors for evangelical communities throughout Germany in the 1530s, Melanchthon had to provide grounds for its actions. He argued that any distinctions between pastors and bishops was a matter of human authority and that "when the regular bishops become enemies of the gospel or are unwilling to ordain, the churches retain their right to do so. For wherever the church exists, there also is the right to administer the gospel. Therefore, it is necessary for the church to retain the right to call, choose, and ordain ministers."[24] In light of current debates over such matters, it is important to note several things. First, the term "regular bishops" is the technical designation of bishops in communion with Rome. During the Reformation, the problem was the authority of the pope not so much the seniority of the bishops or historical succession. Second, the only basis for breaking with such bishops was and is always the gospel itself. Anything less defies that very gospel. Third, the authority to ordain rests not with the congregation or the presbytery but with the churches and the gospel and is a gift from God. That is, in the clause, "when regular bishops become enemies," one could insert "pastors," "synods," or "congregations" as well. *How* Christians order such matters is up to the church to decide. *Whether* they order such matters is not up to them but is mandated by the gospel.

Luther on the Marks of the Church in *The Book of Concord*

Luther's contributions to the question of the marks of the church in those documents of *The Book of Concord* that he authored should be no surprise. First, they match in general what he expressed already in his remarks of 1521. Second, they do not use the term *notae*. Third, they demonstrate Luther's lively concern for the life of the church and the comfort of the gospel. His reflection on the church's marks arose out of his pastoral theology, in the broadest sense of the term.

The Catechisms

Luther did not mention the marks of the church expressly in the catechisms, and yet the concept permeated everything he had to say. In the SC, he tied together an individual's faith with all believers ("just as he calls, gathers, enlightens, and makes holy the whole Christian church on earth and keeps it with Jesus Christ in the one common, true faith").[25] He added one verb ("gathers") to the Holy Spirit's activity and linked it to the gospel, the means by which the Holy Spirit works. The tie to the marks of the church continues in the next phrase. "Daily in this Christian church the Holy Spirit abundantly forgives all sins— mine and those of all believers." In this nonpolemical setting, however, there was no need for Luther to explain the marks—he simply assumed them and used them as the creed itself gave him leave. Already in a sermon on the creed from 1523, Luther made clear the connection between forgiveness and the church.[26] The church must have a sign whereby Christians may recognize it. The phrase in the creed, "forgiveness of sins" comprehends baptism, the Lord's Supper, and confession, the very signs of a living church.

In the Large Catechism, Luther presented a much fuller view of his ecclesiology. He began by noting the links, contained in the creed itself, between the Holy Spirit's work (to make us holy) and the church, forgiveness, and eternal life—the means by which the Holy Spirit does that work. Luther turned first to the church, which he defined for his readers as "a unique community *(Gemeinde)* in the world, which is the mother that begets and bears every Christian through the Word of God."[27] Already in the earliest description of the marks of the church, he had employed the language of begetting. He immediately defined the Word as that "which the Holy Spirit reveals and proclaims, through which he illuminates and inflames hearts so that they grasp and accept it, cling to it, and persevere in it."[28]

He used these basic connections to criticize life under the papacy, where faith and the gospel were "swept under the rug and no one recognized Christ as the Lord or the Holy Spirit as the one who makes us holy."[29] What was lacking? The Holy Spirit! "For where Christ is not preached, there is no Holy Spirit to create, call, and gather the Christian church, apart from which no one can come to the Lord Christ."[30] Here the marks of the church play a crucial role in Luther's thinking. The mark of the Holy Spirit's presence is the preaching of Christ, the means the Holy Spirit uses to create, call, and gather the church. Thus, when Luther accepted Cyprian's famous dictum, *extra ecclesiam nulla salus* (no salvation outside the church), he bound neither salvation nor the church to particular persons and organizations but to the word of God alone. Where Christ is preached, there the Holy Spirit is, and hence there church happens.

After stating that this introduction sufficed, Luther realized that he had to explain some confusing words in this article of the creed, especially *communio sanctorum*. Had he known of modern interpretations, namely, that the phrase may mean participation in holy things (the sacraments), he might not have had to go to such lengths. However, he took the words as equivalent to "holy Christian church." This allowed him to explain the meaning of these phrases more precisely. The word *ecclesia,* he correctly noted, means "assembly" in German. The German word *Kirche,* like the English word "church," comes from the word *kyria* in Greek. It is best rendered as "a Christian community or assembly." It is not architecture. As the modern Christian song goes, "The church is not a building, a committee, or a board. . . . We are the church . . . called, enlightened, sanctified for the work of Jesus Christ."[31] Similarly, Luther linked the word *communio* with community. Thus, the creed speaks of a community of saints or, better, a holy community.

This investigation of these words evoked from Luther one of the more lyrical passages in the Large Catechism.

> I believe that there is on earth a holy little flock and community of pure saints under one head, Christ. It is called together by the Holy Spirit in one faith, mind, and understanding. It possesses a variety of gifts, and yet is united in love without sect or schism. Of this community I also am a part and member, a participant and co-partner in all the blessings it possesses. I was brought into it by the Holy Spirit and incorporated into it through the fact that I have heard and still hear God's Word, which is the beginning point for entering it. Before we had come into this community, we were entirely of the devil, knowing nothing of God and of Christ. The Holy Spirit will remain with the holy community or Christian people until the Last Day. Through it, he gathers us, using it to teach and preach the Word. By it, he creates and increases holiness, causing it daily to grow and become strong in the faith and in its fruits, which the Spirit produces.[32]

It is clear here that Luther was not thinking of some isolated congregations or of their aggregate. The unity comes through the Holy Spirit and the word and links all Christians of every time and place. Moreover, Luther did not tie this church or its unity to any particular definition of hierarchy—congregational, presbyteral, episcopal, or any other kind human beings may cook up. The church, like a snowstorm, is an act of God, who uses the word and sacraments to gather people together. For example, in 1959, my father was in India as an advisor to the government of India and Prime Minister Nehru through the Ford Foundation. After several months, he was so lonely for Christian community that he went to a former Anglican Church, now the Church of North India. Although he did not understand a word of Hindi, he later described to us just how fulfilling it was. He could figure out where they were in the worship and in his head recited the words of the liturgy. Such an experience depicts the nature of Christian unity brought by the Holy Spirit through the word of God. As long as a person knows where he or she is, so to speak, the comfort of the Holy Spirit in the fellowship of believers is also there.

The Smalcald Articles

Luther also discussed the marks of the church in the Smalcald Articles, a document written in 1536 as Luther's theological testament for an impending church council called by the pope to meet in Mantua. After defining word and sacraments in SA III.2–11, Luther turned in SA III.12.1–3 to the church. Speaking specifically of the Roman opponents and their attempt to destroy the Reformation by holding a council, Luther states, "We do not concede to them that they are the church, and frankly they are not the church."[33] Why did he begin in what today would be labeled an unecumenical manner? For basic, ecumenical reasons! The Roman claim to be church eliminated all others not in communion with them and reduced the church to an assembly of bishops in communion with Rome—regardless of whether the gospel is there or not. Luther's intention becomes clear in the next sentence. "We do not want to hear what they command or forbid in the name of the church."[34]

For all the deep flaws in the Joint Declaration on the Doctrine of Justification between Lutherans and Roman Catholics, signed by the Lutheran World Federation and a representative of the pope in Augsburg in 1999, the one saving grace (which nearly sank the document) is the fact that Lutherans did not agree to it because the pope said so but by virtue of the document's own statements about the gospel. The very lack of an ecclesiological principle in that document places Roman ecclesiology in a much more weakened position than many have realized. To have Rome declare anything on the basis of their understanding of the gospel rather than on the basis of some claim of God-given authority is remarkable.

What follows in the Smalcald Articles is then a definition of church that does not depend upon place or person. "God be praised," Luther wrote, "a seven-year-old child knows what the church is: holy believers and 'the little sheep who hear the voice of their shepherd.'"[35] How could he say a child knows this? They recite the creed as an article of faith ("I believe")! Despite the fact that Luther dictated this from what he thought would be his deathbed—he had just suffered a heart attack—these few words contain a wealth of information. First, echoing his interpretation of the creed in the Large Catechism, where he linked the Holy Spirit and the communion of saints, he again used the word "holy." Then, central to his definition, he included the word "believers." This linked the church squarely to faith. His gloss on this first definition gave an even richer texture to the definition. The "little sheep who hear the voice of their shepherd" places the believer under Christ the Good Shepherd (cf. John 10) and in his word ("hear the voice").

Realizing that the word "holy" might be difficult to understand, Luther immediately added an explanation. Holiness is not a matter of monastic dress or other humanly invented ceremonies. The church's holiness "exists in the Word of God and true faith."[36] Here, as in the Large Catechism, Luther linked holiness, one of the adjectives used to modify the word "church" in the Creed, with the word and faith. Only when Christians abandon that God-given word and faith for the self-absorbed holiness of pietism—in whatever form they dream up—do they exchange the true marks of the church for human works and schemes.[37] Thus, as stated above, Luther's understanding of church arose out of his understanding of justification and led back into it. No wonder that in the next article he discussed justification and good works and that in the second part he moved from Christ's work to an attack on the papacy!

The Formula of Concord

At first glance, it would appear that the Formula contains no discussion of the church or its marks whatsoever. In part, this is a tribute to the fundamental agreement between Luther and Melanchthon on this issue and the clarity with which they spoke about it. It simply never came up for discussion in intra-Lutheran controversies—directly, that is. In fact, at least two of the articles, X and XII, contain some indirect references to the common Lutheran ecclesiology outlined in this book. In the course of rejecting Anabaptist positions, article XII renounces any notion of church connected to person or place. Thus, the Concordists rejected the puritanical definition of church in terms of the holiness of persons, namely, "That a congregation or assembly in which sinners are still found is not a true Christian congregation."[38] In the next sentence, they dismissed any tie to place, "that no one should attend or hear a sermon in houses of worship in which papistic Masses were previously recited."[39] As they concluded, "the entire sect is basically nothing else than a new monasticism."[40] This always happens where church is divorced from the marks of word and sacrament and forced to dream up its own, humanly generated, marks.

Article X deals with the question of adiaphora. Here, the Concordists produced a kind of commentary on CA XV and the question of human traditions. They even titled it "Concerning Ecclesiastical Practices."[41] Unlike Melanchthon, whose behavior in this matter just after the defeat of the evangelical princes in the Smalcald War left much to be desired in the eyes of some Lutherans, the Concordists decided that in the face of direct persecution things that were adiaphora suddenly became matters demanding confession of faith.

For both Luther and Melanchthon, only the word made demands on Christians. Everything else remained *indifferentia,* to use the Latin equivalent of the Greek adiaphora. The aftermath of the Smalcald War revealed that under certain, limited circumstances, indifferent matters, when forced upon Christians by enemies of the gospel, did not remain indifferent. In fact, this article is a handy summary of how to sort out disagreements in the church. Born out of a potential fracture among Lutherans, this article reveals the Concordists' blueprint for resolving church disputes. The church today could profit from their advice.

What do Christians learn here about the marks of the church? First, and in the present situation foremost, it is important to realize that such opposition to adiaphora comes up only when faced with enemies of the gospel. Such thoughts as, "We've never done it that way," or "I don't want to change," or "I don't like the way the vote went" do not qualify. One must first demonstrate beyond any doubt that some change in practice has arisen out of the persecution by enemies—*enemies*—of the gospel.

Second, the Formula clearly defines such indifferent matters. They are not the gospel but are introduced into the churches "for the sake of good order and decorum."[42] To be sure, they are not inconsequential things, yet none should be confused with *Gottesdienst,* that is, service to and worship of God. For example, several years ago the ELCA bishops of region seven (from Eastern Pennsylvania through New England) met with the faculty of the Lutheran Theological Seminary at Philadelphia and urged a restatement of its support for Called to Common Mission (CCM), the agreement between the ELCA and the Episcopal Church. Bishop after bishop—I remember especially comments by bishops Lee Miller and Roy Riley—stood up and talked about the ways in which this agreement would help them do mission in the Northeast. That is, they understood the agreement as part of the "good order and decorum" that should measure all such matters.

Third, the community of God has authority to alter such indifferent matters as it sees fit. We are not stuck in a particular past nor enthralled to certain persons or places. "The community of God in every place and at every time has the authority to alter such ceremonies according to its own situation, as may be most useful and edifying for the community of God."[43] Christian leaders must simply ask how useful it is for the church. No other measure, save the gospel itself, matters.

Fourth, the Formula warns against offending the weak.[44] How many times have well-intended but foolish changes in practice imposed on the weak by overzealous pastors or laypersons rent congregations asunder? How many times have well-intended but foolish refusals to alter old practices imposed on the weak by overly cautious pastors or laypersons rent congregations asunder? Sometimes this happens in entire church bodies as well. The Concordists put the churches on notice always to look out for the weak.

Finally, after a description of what must take place under persecution, the Concordists added a reference to Irenaeus, who purportedly said, "Dissimilarity in fasting is not to disrupt unity in faith."[45] They did this to preserve a central aspect of adiaphora. "No church should condemn another because the one has fewer or more external ceremonies not commanded by God than the other has, when otherwise there is unity with the other in teaching and all the articles of faith and in the proper use of the holy sacraments."[46] That is why the most important section of CCM is the one over which no one has much argued: paragraph five, where the basic agreement in doctrine is outlined, much of it using the language of the CA itself! Once we have achieved agreement in the marks of the church—word and sacraments—then these other matters become indifferent. Then the debate must turn not over good and evil but over what best serves and edifies the church and protects the weak.

This chapter has shown how Luther's basic insights into the ecumenical nature of the church and its marks influenced Lutheran confessional documents. Perhaps Christians can use their testimony to strengthen an ecumenical witness to the gospel of Jesus Christ. Sometimes one wonders, however, whether this definition of church gives Christians so much freedom in the gospel that we just cannot bear it. We prefer to creep back to the fleshpots of Egypt than stand in the liberating word of Christ that daily creates a church of forgiven sinners, marked by the voice of the Shepherd and his signs of forgiveness, concord, and love.

Chapter 5

The Marks of the Church in the Later Luther

This chapter continues an examination of the historical record with an eye toward how the reformers' concept of marks of the church may inform modern ecclesiology. In some ways, the results of this chapter were already anticipated in chapter 3, where a variety of Lutherans from different times and places bore witness to the lively tradition of the church's marks. Moreover, this chapter demonstrates how the confessional tradition, discussed in the previous chapter, far from restricting or narrowing Lutheran ecclesiology, remained in the hands of its main proponents, Luther and Melanchthon, a vital, growing center of theological reflection.

Thus, this chapter will take a more integrated approach and summarize how the marks of the church function in Luther's writings after 1521, paying special attention to two important texts, excerpts of which appear in this book's appendixes. One represents a joint effort of Melanchthon and Luther in an academic disputation granting Johannes Macchabäus a degree in 1542, and the other is a sermon of Luther on the baptism of Jesus from 1544. Taken together, they demonstrate how flexible the concept of *notae ecclesiae* was in Luther's thought and how this category functioned within the broader scope of Lutheran theology.

Marks of the Church in the Later Luther (1523–46)

Although Luther's concept of the marks of the church arose in a particular polemical context, he continued to use the notion throughout his career.[1] In part, he did this because the opponents kept harping on what they considered his defective ecclesiology. For example, John Eck—one of Luther's harshest critics—in one of his most popular works, the *Enchiridion,* used Matthew 18 and Christ's command to "tell it to the church" against Luther's notion of the hidden, spiritual church.

> If the church is hidden, how did Christ command us to "tell it to the church"? If it were hidden, what could be said to it, or how would it hear? . . . Let Luther say whether they were hidden and only mathematically the Church, when Paul said, "Now you are the body of Christ, and individually members of it."[2]

Luther and Melanchthon had to respond to this kind of polemic throughout their lives. Failure to respond, in their day or today, invariably results in a return to an ecclesiology of place and person.

Defining the Church by Its Marks

When Luther taught, preached, and wrote about the church, the notion of its marks was always close at hand. Many times he simply assumed the church had marks and used the concept. At least once, however, while lecturing on Psalm 90 in 1534, he provided an exposition of the term in a discussion of v. 1, "Lord, you have been our dwelling place throughout all generations."

> Therefore when you are minded to pass judgment on the church, you must not look for a church in which there are no blemishes and flagrant faults, but for one where the pure Word of God is present, where there is the right administration of the Sacraments, and where there are people who love the Word and confess it before others. Where you discover these earmarks, there you may be sure the church exists, whether the number of those who have and observe these earmarks is small or whether the number is large. We are certain that there will always be some who are members of the church. Otherwise, how could God have been our Dwelling Place from eternity?[3]

The next sections will discuss the specific marks and the weakness of the church. For now, it is important to note Luther's use of the term "earmarks" (German: *Kennzeichen*), which is a good German rendering of the Latin term *notae*. Furthermore, Luther joined to the standard marks of word and sacrament another kind of mark: the effect of word and sacraments among believers, namely, love of the word and confession of faith in that word. Most importantly, the purpose of the marks is to offer the believer assurance that God has not abandoned us.

Throughout his career, Luther continued to use a variety of words for the marks of the church, another sign that this was a new concept for him and thus not terminologically fixed. One of the most creative terms for these marks came in a sermon on Maundy Thursday from 1538. In comments on the foot washing, Luther stated,

> Let us see to it that we discern the church by its colors. The first is the Gospel with the Lord's Supper, confession of Christ and Baptism, that is, the characteristic markings [*Merckzeichen*]. The second is the footwashing, not simply externally but even more excellently everyone as servant to the other. These are inborn in Christians from birth. Christian things are not recognized by their hats but by these two signs: where Christians believe in Christ and are saved by faith and where they humbly give themselves to one another.[4]

Colors, markings, signs! Here Luther did not deny that, as the song goes, "They will know we are Christians by our love," but he was also careful to give preeminence to the word and sacraments and the faith that word creates. The text of John 13, however, forced him to include love as a fruit of that faith. This sermon demonstrates Luther's deep commitment the notion of the *notae ecclesiae*. In this case, when confronted with a clear word of Christ ("By this they shall know you are my disciples, that you love one another"), Luther did not abandon his own definition of the Christian's "colors" but simply tacked Jesus' sign (love) onto his own (the word and faith).

Luther's Lists of Marks

In the writings of both Luther and Melanchthon, the list of the church's marks varied, with one of the most complete lists coming in Luther's tract on the church in 1539.[5] Different situations or, as demonstrated above, different biblical texts gave rise to different lists. However, all invariably went back to the word and the sacraments (visible words) and their effects on the Christian community (confession of faith and love).

The Centrality of the Word

Luther always gave priority to the word of God or the gospel. There are several reasons for this. For one thing, he understood God to have created the world through the word and to re-create believers through the same word. For another, he viewed the sacraments as visible words. Finally, he always tied the church to faith (the assembly of believers) and thus stressed the Pauline notion that faith comes by hearing (Rom. 10:17). In all this, Luther was thinking not about a word in a book but about a living, spoken word—in fact, the word of Christ.

In his 1523 tract *Concerning the Ministry,* written to the Bohemian church, he defined the duties of bishop in terms of the word and added, "A church is not known by customs but by the Word."[6] For those who are uncertain whether they are members of the church, he added, "Stand fast then, good sirs, and go forth with the Word of God, armed with the invincible and all-powerful sword of the Spirit."[7]

Four years later, in lectures on Isaiah, first published in the mid-1530s, he discussed Isa. 2:3 ("Out of Zion shall go forth instruction, and the word of the Lord from Jerusalem"). He referred to Romans 10 and added, "By the Word alone, therefore, the Church is recognized, and in the glory of the Word the reign of Christ is described."[8] Luther preferred always to speak of the word alone, rather than scripture alone, because it implied a living, spoken word (Rom. 10:17: "Faith comes by hearing").

In 1533, Luther insisted that Lutherans were not heretics, "for we have, God be praised, the Word of God in its purity and certainty, as the pope does not have it." He then linked this Word to the other marks of the church. "However, where God's word is pure and certain, there everything else must be: God's kingdom, Christ's kingdom, the Holy Spirit, baptism, the sacrament [of the Lord's Supper], the office of ministry, the office of preaching, faith, love, the cross, life and salvation, and everything the church should have."[9]

Confession of Faith

Already in the lectures on Psalm 90, Luther mentioned confession of faith in his definition of the marks of the church. This, too, he connected with Romans 10 and justification by faith. He had already noticed this mark in 1531, in lectures on Psalm 22 published posthumously in 1551. There, in a longer list of manifest signs *(signa monstrantia)*,[10] he had included confession [of faith], the cross, and prayer. This mark, especially as it became associated with the ancient creeds, imparted an ecumenical thrust to Luther's understanding of the church. Such public confession of Christ also moved quite naturally to the cross and persecution for the faith, part of the evangelical Christian experience during the Reformation.

The Catechism

Luther linked the catechism to the marks of the church in a sermon on John 16 from 9 May 1535. In reflecting on Jesus' prediction of persecution, Luther insisted that the evangelicals were not heretics. In fact, their opponents had to admit that they had all the signs of the church. "They know well that we preach the gospel of Christ. . . . We teach correctly concerning baptism, the Sacrament [of the Altar], the Gospel. The simple catechism (that is, the Our Father and the creed) is accessible."[11] By mentioning the catechism, Luther brought the marks of the church into each Wittenberg household, putting in each person's hands the word, sacraments, and prayer. Perhaps the penchant for making the Bible and theology complicated and, hence, inaccessible, may best be cured by returning permanently to the basics of the Ten Commandments, the Apostles' Creed, the Lord's Prayer, and the sacraments—not simply as a one-shot deal, this year's "mission emphasis." Finally, the reason for basic catechesis in the church is the same as the reason for preaching and providing the sacraments; it, too, marks the church.

Prayer

Whereas in Ap VII/VIII Melanchthon listed *answered* prayer as a gift of the Holy Spirit to the church, Luther made prayer itself a mark of the church in the same year the Apology was being written, 1531. The Lord's Prayer is, of course, a part of the catechism. However, prayer also marks the church because, like confession, it is a fruit of faith, where faith itself comes to life through the word. Prayer is simply faith breathing. As Luther put it in the Large Catechism, God commands us to pray, promises to hear us, and furnishes the words to say, the Lord's Prayer, which comprehends all a Christian needs. "The true church is the one which prays."[12] Of course, Luther was not referring to the "babbling and bellowing" that still passes for prayer today.[13] Rather, he had in mind the cry of the blind Timaeus outside Jericho, the church's continual *Kyrie eleison* that echoes throughout the centuries. One of the surest signs of the true church came on the last words Luther wrote, "We are beggars; this is true."[14]

Ordination

The 1539 treatise on the church was not the first place that Luther discussed ordination as a mark of the church. Already in 1531, Melanchthon had argued in Ap XIII that under certain circumstances the evangelical side could consider ordination to word and sacrament ministry as a sacrament.[15] With the onset of regular ordinations in Wittenberg in the 1530s, Luther had even more reason to include this mark. It is by no means a mere exception that he discussed it in his 1539 treatise on the church.

In 1533, Luther listed the offices of ministry and preaching as marks of the church and included a brief description of ordination as the function of true bishops and pastors.

> The same little pastor or bishop, St. Augustine, consecrated and ordained many pastors or bishops in his little parish (since they were not yet consecrating bishops or archbishops but nothing but pastors), who were sought and called by other cities, as we ordain and send them out of our parish at Wittenberg to other cities which want them and do not have any pastors among them. For ordaining should consist of and be understood as calling to and entrusting with the office of the ministry. Christ and his church, wherever it is in the world, have and must have this power, without chrism and tonsure, just as they must have the word, baptism, the sacrament [of the Lord's Supper], the Spirit, and faith.[16]

Again, in his lectures on Genesis from the same time, Luther discussed the meaning of Jacob's ladder and his naming the place "House of God" and "Gate of Heaven." He began with the (now) standard definition of the church's marks. "Wherever that Word is heard, where Baptism, the Sacrament of the Altar, and absolution are administered, there you must determine and conclude with certainty: 'This is surely God's house; here heaven has been opened.'"[17] In later comments on the same verse, however, he rejected the notion that churches were simply stone buildings and insisted instead that they are marked by the word. "But when sermons are delivered [in such buildings], when the sacraments are administered and ministers are ordained to teach, then say: 'Here is the house of God and gate of heaven; for God is speaking. . . .'"[18] Not only the sermons themselves but the act of setting persons aside to deliver them and to teach constituted a mark of the church.

Luther went even further. The notion of the ladder coming down from heaven led him to reflect on the incarnation and the great contrast between the word of God and the ministerial vessels in which it comes. In later years, he often expressed what modern theologians call the theology of the cross—the revelation of God in the last place you or I would reasonably look—in terms of the humanity and brokenness of the church.[19]

> It is great honor and majesty, however, when one says: "This is the Word of God." I hear a human voice. I see human gestures. The bread and the wine in the Supper are physical things. At ordination the hands of carnal folks are imposed. In Baptism water is water. For the flesh judges in no other way concerning all these matters. But if you look at that addition with spiritual eyes, namely, at whose Word it is that is spoken and heard there, not indeed a human word—for if it is that, then the devil is speaking—but the Word of God, then you will understand that it is the house of God and the gate of heaven.[20]

After looking in detail at the Sacrament of Baptism and contrasting it to the Anabaptist understanding, he returned to ordination. "Thus, the imposition of hands is not a human tradition, but God makes and ordains ministers."[21] For Luther, the marks of the church were hardly imposing—bread and wine, water, hands. What made the difference was the word of God, that is, God's promise to do what the words and actions declared.

Cross

Although this mark, too, appeared in the 1539 treatise on the church, Luther referred to this a good deal more often. Already in 1523, in his remarks to the Bohemian church on the ministry, he noted that if evangelical preaching and consecration were instituted in the church of his day, "we must reckon with a cross."[22] In many ways, this mark was an extension of the preceding sections, in that Luther was now developing what might be called an ecclesiology of the cross. It also reflected Wittenberg's realization that the papal party wanted nothing less than the elimination of the evangelicals. Again, in comments on Psalm 22 from 1531, he already mentioned the cross as one of the marks of the church.[23] He went into more detail in his lectures on Genesis. In comments on Abel, Luther, like Melanchthon, connected persecution by the godless, who claim the name church, to Rom. 8:29 and Paul's remarks on being conformed to Christ ("for your sake we are being slain"). "Therefore the true church is hidden; it is banned; it is regarded as heretical; it is slain."[24] Emphasizing this mark had important ramifications for the later development of the marks of the church.

The fact that Luther moved so effortlessly from the murder of Abel by Cain to the persecution of the church may surprise modern readers of scripture. Not only did this reflect the exegetical tradition, but it also underscored Luther's belief, mentioned above, that the church had existed in all ages, always revealed *sub contrario specie,* hidden in weakness. Thus, in a discussion of the pre-Abrahamic patriarchs, Luther insisted: "Can there be any doubt that the holy fathers always had their gatherings and meetings, when they instructed the youth, where they preached, prayed, prophesied, and praised God? The church cannot exist without the constant use of the Word, and the church always had its sacraments, or tokens of grace, and its ceremonies."[25]

Some of the behavior in today's church comes from a fatal unbelief, what one person has called functional atheism.[26] Deep down Christians fear that God has abandoned them and will not continue to see to the proclamation of the word and the strengthening of faith in the church. Faith alone can turn such atheists back into believers. If the church survived Cain killing Abel, it can probably survive present-day shenanigans, too.

Signs of the Church—Signs of God's Presence

As discussed in a previous chapter, by often using the term "signs" for the marks of the church, Luther forged an indissoluble bond between the sacraments and the marks. Moreover, this immediately allowed him to connect his sacramental theology to his ecclesiology. In part, this arose by linking the theology of the cross with the sacraments. He also insisted—always with a critical eye cocked toward the Anabaptists and the followers of Ulrich Zwingli—that God always works through signs. In a 1531 sermon on Pentecost, he noted the tongues of fire and reminded his hearers, "In this way, whenever the Holy Spirit is to begin a Christian church, he must show himself externally with a sign, so that it may be comprehended."[27]

At the same time, Luther linked the signs of the church to signs of God's presence. Thus, the *notae* really are signs of (God's!) life. *God* speaks, baptizes, celebrates the supper, and ordains. Luther made this connection in his discussion of Psalm 90, which proclaimed God as "our dwelling place." In lectures on Psalm 121 from 1532/33, he remarked, "Now the name of God dwells in Christ. Where Christ is, there is the church. Where the word of Christ, the Sacrament [of the Lord's Supper], Baptism, and prayer are, those are our hills."[28]

In lectures on Gen. 15:13-16, God's prophecy to Abraham that his descendants would be slaves in Egypt evoked this comment on God's presence in the church.

> The Turkish religion and the papacy are most powerful monsters. In recent times the church has been severely afflicted by them; yet amid the ragings of the dragon and the lion Baptism remains, the Eucharist remains, the power of the Keys remains, and the text of the Bible, or Holy Scripture, remains. Certainly this is not through human power; otherwise the Turk and the pope would have long since done away with these. But through

his power God preserves these, so that when the Word and the sacraments remain, faith and the church remain in spite of the pope and the Turk.[29]

Human power would in Luther's eyes always fail. God, however, remained with the church through its marks. In Luther's thought, these three things always coalesce: word, enemies, and a weak church. Thus, in one of his most beloved hymns, he prayed first, "Keep us steadfast in your word," but followed that immediately with "Restrain the murderous pope and Turk." This represented not saber rattling, theological triumphalism, but quite the opposite, a confession that God alone rules the church. Thus, in the second verse he begs Christ to use his power to defend his "poor Christendom" (that is, "lowly church" and not, as the standard translation reads, "holy church").[30]

The Hidden, Persecuted, Sinning Church

The idea that the church is hidden is an old one. Already Augustine, in his arguments against the Donatists, had insisted that the visible church contains a mixture of weeds and wheat, sinner and saint. He and later theologians developed the notion of the invisible church, knit together into the mystical body of Christ with Christ himself as the head. To be sure, some of these ideas influenced Luther's ecclesiology. However, justification by faith alone led him to speak about the church not as an institution but as the gathering of believers in Christ. When this notion came under attack, Luther then developed the idea of *notae ecclesiae*. However, Luther never stopped developing his own understanding of the hidden church, combining elements of the Augustinian teaching, justification by faith alone, and the theology of the cross to enliven his own ecclesiology.

The Church's Hiddenness as an Article of Faith

First, Luther realized that defining the church as an assembly of believers meant that it was ipso facto hidden. Given the apostasy on the part of the papal party, it would have been tempting to argue that Christ had deserted the church. In a public disputation on the subject of private masses, held in 1536 at Wittenberg as part of a doctoral defense, Luther insisted that Christ had not left the church because of his promise in Matthew 28 to be with us always. Thus, one can find the church among the Greeks and even in the Roman church. How could Luther say this? "The church is seen not with fleshly eyes but with the eyes of faith."[31] That is why we confess that we *believe* in the holy catholic church, because it is not seen, as Heb. 11:1 ("Faith is the conviction of things not seen") states. At this point in the debate, the protocols noted that a distinguished visitor added to Luther's comments. The Anglican bishop Fox from Hereford, who was in Wittenberg (probably for negotiations with the Saxon princes), referred to the account of Elijah that 7,000 had not bowed the knee to Baal as an example of the hidden church. "Thus, he approved the words of Doctor Luther."[32] At least at one time Lutherans and Anglicans agreed on this issue.

The Church Is Hidden in Persecution

As we already saw in his lectures on Genesis, Luther also tied the church's hiddenness to Abel's death and, hence, to persecution. "Therefore the true church is hidden; it is banned; it is regarded as heretical; it is slain." Abel was not just a figure of the true church but stood at its beginning. Reason will always look with disdain at this poor, weak, persecuted gathering of believers. Only faith grasps Christ's promise in the midst of suffering.

The Church Is Hidden under Sin

The church is also hidden under sin. To the Bohemians, Luther wrote in 1523 not only that "we must reckon with a cross," but also that "the church is indeed weak because of its sins. . . . We may not, therefore, reject those who accept and confess the Word, even though they do not shine in any splendid sanctity, as long as they do not persist in manifest sins."[33] Eleven years later, in comments on Psalm 90, he said the same thing. "The church is not a perfectly holy society or completely free of flagrant faults and blemishes, as the Papists imagine it to be."[34] Like the Donatists, Luther's opponents pointed to their own holiness, rather than admitting that we must daily ask God for forgiveness. This mistaken understanding of holiness still mars much of contemporary understanding of the church, especially in the United States.

Taking his cue from Jesus' parable of the weeds and wheat, Luther described the church and its marks in a sermon from 1536. Here, he combined hiddenness, sin, and the word to define his ecclesiology.

> That is, as we often say, the Christian church will exist nowhere except where there are also terrible weeds . . . mixed in with the grain. Whoever looks at the church with its brokenness and rebellious spirits and thinks Christians are not present will miss the church of Christ. Therefore, for us, it is a consolation when the grace and treasure of God are present, as Paul says. Still there are a lot of people around who do not believe in the resurrection of the dead. This does not hurt baptism, only themselves. The gospel, the Lord's Prayer, correct Baptism remain. Therefore, where the word is purely preached, then baptism, absolution, Ten Commandments, Lord's Prayer, and good works can remain pure. Therefore, the greatest treasure remains in the church when the pure word—as we purely hold the word— remains.[35]

In his Genesis lectures, the description in Genesis 32 of Jacob limping away from Bethel led Luther to the following depiction of the church and its marks.

> For what is this whole assembly which is called the church? It is a tiny little flock of the most wretched, forlorn, and hopeless people in the sight of the world. What is this flock compared with the whole world, what is it compared with the kingdom of the Turks and France, indeed, compared even with our adversaries, the papists? So if you asked where the church is, it is nowhere in evidence. But you must not pay regard to external form but to the Word and to Baptism, and the church must be sought where the sacraments are purely administered, where there are hearers, teachers, and confessors of the Word.[36]

This passage demonstrates that late in his career Luther still clung to the notion of the church's hiddenness. However, he now tied it not simply to faith, something which cannot be seen with the eye, but to faith's effects: persecution, weakness, and confession of sin. No wonder that a century later, according to legend, Gustavus Adolphus could lead his troops into battle singing, "O little flock, fear not the foe that proudly seeks your overthrow."

Rome and Wittenberg Are Church

This combination of the church's hiddenness, its persecution, and its sin on the one side with the church's marks on the other led to two opposite effects, both of which influence the ecumenical heart of Lutheranism. On the one hand, Luther insisted that Rome is the church because it had certain marks. On the other, so is Wittenberg. In his widely published and read Galatians lectures of 1535, Luther discussed what it meant that the church is in the midst of a crooked and perverse generation (Phil. 2:15), surrounded by wolves and robbers (John 10).

> Although the city of Rome is worse than Sodom and Gomorra, nevertheless there remain in it Baptism, the Sacrament [of the Altar], the voice and text of the Gospel, the Sacred Scriptures, the ministries, the name of Christ, and the name of God. . . . Therefore, the church of Rome is holy, because it has the holy name of God, the Gospel, Baptism, etc. If these are present among a people, that people is called holy. Thus, this Wittenberg of ours is a holy village, and we are truly holy because we have been baptized, communed, taught and called by God; we have the works of God among us, that is, the Word and the sacraments, and these make us holy.[37]

In comments on Jacob's ladder, discussed above, Luther also insisted that Rome is the church. Despite the struggle with the papists, they are the church because they have baptism, absolution, the text of the gospel, and many godly people among them. Only when they insist that there is no church outside of the Roman pontiff are there grounds for resisting them. "If the church is to be the house of God, it is necessary for it to have the Word of God and for God alone to be the Head of the household in this house."[38] However,

Luther also insisted that by the same measure Wittenberg itself is equally the church. In his sermon on John 16:4 for Exaudi Sunday 1535, he even forced the papal party to admit that, given the presence of the marks of the church, the Wittenbergers could not be heretics.

> For they know we are the true church, because here is true baptism, Gospel, the right administration of the sacrament, faith in the remission of sins, hope of eternal life, the Our Father, the Ten Commandments and all other gifts which pertain to the Christian church and the witness of Christ Jesus. Therefore, it is a true Christian church, and we are in the office.[39]

In the same sermon, Luther touched on two things that often seem to be opposites in the current debate over the church. On the one hand, he reiterated the Saxon position first taken in Augsburg that the evangelicals are willing to submit to the bishops—godless though they may be—provided that they allow them to be pastors and preachers. On the other, he rejected any claim that the pope represents the church. Jesus says where two or three are gathered together, he is there. "If we have the Highest Pontiff [Christ], we can bid the pope good night. . . . Nothing rests in the person." This implies that the person of the minister does not matter. So Luther added, "In an emergency a woman can baptize, and it is a true baptism, although she is not publicly called. Moreover, Christ confirms the baptism, as the churches indicate when they confirm her baptism by the laying on of hands."[40]

The Place of Bishops

In the next breath in this very sermon, Luther stressed the importance of the public ministry. The fact that anyone can exercise the office does not undercut the unique office of ministry. It is that public office that the woman baptizing fills, not some democratic one created by the priesthood of all believers. The Christian church in any circumstance must see to it that that public office remains filled. When the bishops refuse to fill the office with people faithful to the gospel, then the church must take steps to fill it in any case.

This high regard for the public office of ministry in general matched Luther's high regard for the specific, episcopal office of oversight. He counseled the Bohemians in 1523 to establish bishops by gathering the clergy, praying, and electing bishops, and laying hands on them to receive the office of bishop, minister, or pastor. The bishops themselves may then come together and elect one of their number to be archbishop, "who would serve them and hold visitations among them, as Peter visited the churches according to the account in the book of Acts."[41]

Years later, in a tract on the private mass and consecration of priests, he again insisted that Lutherans were not heretics and that the word gave them the right to ordain. However, Luther did not argue on the basis of some sort of presbyteral succession or on some innate authority of the local congregation or the priesthood of all believers. Instead, he insisted that Jerome and Paul held that bishop and pastor are the same thing and that in Augustine's day, "every separate city had a bishop, even as they now have pastors."[42]

True and False Church

In two places in the lectures on Genesis, in texts dealing with Jacob and Esau, Luther contrasted the true and false church. He insisted that this division had plagued the church from the beginning, that is, already in the time of the patriarchs. The heart of the false church was the claim that person and place matter.

> If you ask the pope why he is the people of God, he answers: "Because I am sitting in the seat of the apostles Peter and Paul and am their successor." . . . Even a dog or a swine, however, can sit in the place of St. Peter; but to have the call—that is, the Word which you believe over and above that succession—that, of course, establishes the church and the children of God.[43]

On what basis can a person know where the true church is? Through its marks, of course! "We have the Gospel, Baptism, the Keys, and Holy Scripture, which teaches that humankind is lost and condemned in original sin and that is must be born again through Christ."[44]

In further ruminations of the relation between Jacob and Esau, Luther discussed the marks or "worst colors" of the false church. First, it impudently and proudly misused God's name. Second, it despised the things that belong to the true church, "just as the pope and the bishops do not teach, do not baptize, and do not perform any other duty in the church."[45] This meant, at the same time, that Christians could tolerate bad, even godless pastors who nevertheless performed their office according to the word.

> I can put up with it when someone is a Christian in number only and meanwhile still performs the outward duty. Even if he is secretly godless and vicious, there is nothing to prevent one from calling him a Christian or the church in number, but not worth—provided that he baptizes, takes care of the sick, and strengthens troubled consciences.[46]

A third mark (or worst color, as Luther put it) of the false church is that it hankers after the pleasures and glory of this life. A final mark is contempt for the promise of God in their lives. All four visibly mark the false church for what it was: an assembly of unbelievers who trust themselves not God's promising Word.

The Disputation of Johannes Macchabäus, 1542

In the Middle Ages and through the Reformation, every degree granted by a university came only after the candidate had undergone public questioning, which was called a disputation and based upon theses that he and his teachers had formulated. One such disputation took place on 3 February 1542 for the promotion to doctor of theology of a Scotsman Ian, whom Philip Melanchthon had nicknamed in Latin Johannes Macchabäus.[47] Although Melanchthon formulated the theses, they were defended in the theological faculty under the presidency of Martin Luther. Thus, the theses, the majority of which deal directly with evangelical ecclesiology, give a glimpse into the mature thought on the church by both men.

Melanchthon's Theses[48]

The first nine theses dealt directly with an evangelical understanding of the church. Right off the bat, Melanchthon defined the subject for debate. First, the *visible* church (as opposed to the hidden church uniting all believers) includes hypocrites and unbelievers. This truth is so often missing from instruction of congregations and synods today that modern churches operate on the assumption that if the church would only get its act together, it could be rid of all sinners and hypocrites and succeed. This addiction to purity (or success, a peculiarly American form of purity) simply distorts the gospel of the forgiveness of sins.

Second, besides the mixture of saints and sinners, the church agrees in true doctrine—a trait demonstrated by external characteristics *(notae)*: pure gospel and legitimate sacraments. Thus, in the second thesis Melanchthon defined justification by faith alone in a manner typical of his later thought, so that it included faith, regeneration, and the fruits of faith. It simply clarified the term "saint" in the preceding thesis.

The third thesis explained why the term "gospel" came up in thesis one and contrasted this to "the ordinary succession of bishops." The question here was *not* whether the church has or does not have such succession—that is adiaphora—but whether it is *bound* to such a succession. Any Lutheran who imagines that the Lutheran church was somehow incomplete or not fully church without such succession must deny that in 1542 the church in Wittenberg was church![49] Luther and Melanchthon were not willing to do that. The question was what has priority in the church: its political survival or the gospel. According to Melanchthon the church stood under the marching orders of the voice at the Mount of Transfiguration: "Listen to him!" It is bound to no one else in the same way. The voice of God from the cloud did not say, "This is my beloved Peter, James, or John," but "This is my beloved Son; listen to him." That verse is crucial for evangelical ecclesiology. The reformers cited it constantly. Luther's sermons on the text often contrasted papal claims (and, by extension, claims of those bishops in communion with Rome) to this command.

The crucial word in this context is "bound" *(alligata est)*. From the beginning, what marked evangelical ecclesiology (as opposed to either Roman or Reformed ecclesiology) was the enormous sense of freedom that arises directly out of the word of God and God's command, "Listen to him!" One could easily rewrite this thesis to contrast the voice from the cloud to those who bind the church, say, to a particular seminary faculty or teacher, to any congregation (or all of them), to the local pastor or presbytery. The church is bound, *bound,* only to the gospel of Jesus Christ. His word, as professed in the church's teaching and preaching the gospel and in the legitimate use of the sacraments, binds it to the word as to nothing else on earth. In comparison to the gospel itself, all else *must* be adiaphora or *indifferentia.*

At present, this perspective is crucial in order to *legitimate* episcopal authority in the church. No one can dismiss bishops out of hand, even if a church switches from a congregational polity to an episcopal one. Thesis four makes that abundantly clear. A rejection of any polity in any church must begin with the phrase, "When bishops [or fill in the blank with any other human authority] oppose the gospel. . . ." Without that phrase (whether lacking in documents of proponents or opponents to historical succession), the debate pits not Christian versus Christian but episcopal papist versus congregational (or presbyteral or individual) papist. Moreover, the curse upon such people comes not from the church or believers at all but from God ("cursed by divine judgment"). In fact, the church does not do whatever it wants, but "divine command" forces it to leave such errant bishops. The "anathema" Melanchthon explained as exclusion from the church, rejection of them, and avoidance of their contagion.

Melanchthon's use of Gal. 1:8 in thesis four stood in a twenty-two-year history of evangelical usage in this context, beginning with Luther's defense against Rome, especially at the Diet of Worms.[50] It underscored the point that breaking with bishops is *never* done because there is something wrong with bishops per se, but because of the gospel alone. The church is bound to the gospel. Therefore, when and only when bishops oppose the gospel, must evangelical Christians separate themselves from them. Then they do not have a choice, and they cannot base their ecclesiology upon that separation but only upon the gospel. However, if the gospel itself is not at stake, then such separation is simply schismatic.[51]

In theses five to eight, Melanchthon contrasted governmental succession and the church's succession. By using a highly nuanced version of the doctrine of the two kingdoms, he provided a new way to gain perspective on succession of any kind in the church. Thesis five describes human governments in terms of succession, power to interpret laws, distinctions among persons (with some of higher and lower rank), and (in sum) glory. The church, Melanchthon argued in thesis six, possesses none of these traits. The word church, in the first instance, does not denote a political entity but a "dispersed body." It has no leader, no power, and no human glory. This definition puts the lie not simply to exaggerated claims of bishops, but also to similar claims by individuals, pastors, congregations, synods, or churchwide entities. Anytime we define church in terms of such things, we are no longer talking about church in this sense at all but about some sort of government. Now, it may be an ecclesiastical government, but it is not church.

Having rejected kingship, power, and glory for the church in thesis six, Melanchthon now suddenly reintroduced the same three terms in thesis seven, claiming that the church had all three but now defining them in very different ways. First, he argued that the head of the church is Christ. Much of what goes on in today's churches contradicts this fundamental truth. Permeating our ecclesial life is the plague of "functional atheism," that is, the conviction that God is not active in daily life. Second, Melanchthon turned the word "glory" on its head. The glory of God does not describe how we give glory to God but how God reveals glory and makes us glorious. Finally, there are great feats *(res gestae)* among Christians. This glory does not have to do with victories in synod assemblies or congregational meetings but with our struggle against the devil—a war to the death. (Melanchthon is so intent on succinctly describing this battle that he even imports a Greek adjective that means "afforded no truce" to portray the war.)

It is, however, thesis eight that contains perhaps the biggest surprise of all. "In the church there must be judgments *(iudicia)*." Here

Melanchthon was picking up not only on the question of harmony in the church but also on the notion of governmental judging of laws mentioned in thesis five. Harmony in the visible church is not a Platonic dream; it is a perceivable reality. The church actually has the gift of interpreting scripture. Even this gift, however, cannot be tied to or guaranteed by a particular office. This gift remains inextricably bound to the word itself and can never be subsumed under a particular office: whether that office is bishop, congregation, pastor, synod, or churchwide assembly, or any other humanly constructed authority.

Melanchthon finally resolved this ambiguity in the ninth thesis. Here it is clear that Melanchthon meant to say that there is a real gift of interpreting scripture and that the church must somehow make judgments about good and bad doctrine. The only reason the Wittenberg church could not follow the ordinary bishops of his day came from the Word of God, which convicted them of idolmania (one of Melanchthon's favorite terms). Thus, his discussion of church and authority in the church had to move from formal definitions to specific doctrines. In the remaining theses (ten to twenty-four) he convicted these bishops of false doctrine. *Only* on that basis could the church reject their authority. As Luther then pointed out in the subsequent debate, the same was true of the "bishop" of Wittenberg, Johannes Bugenhagen. Were his successors to teach heresy, the church would have to reject them, too.

The Disputation

The disputation itself returned to several of the themes struck in the theses. Here not only Macchabäus but also Luther and perhaps even Melanchthon himself gave voice to some of their chief concerns about the nature of the church.

Obedience to Superiors in the Church: Based upon the Gospel
First, on the question of obedience to superiors in the church, as commanded by Heb. 13:7, Luther made the following argument. He accepted the fact that there must be such superiors and that Christians owe them obedience. For those who confuse democracy with church polity, this may come as a shock. Luther then insisted that

Christians owed obedience to these superiors precisely because they care for souls. This alone also provided the rationale for disobedience. "However, in this way I accept the major premise but deny the minor. For our bishops are not vigilant for us but are rather pernicious wolves, attacking the consciences of souls. They are vigilant instead that souls may perish rather than be saved. They do not exercise care of souls."[52]

The Church: Visible and Hidden in the Flesh

On the visible nature of the church, the thought of the two reformers seemed to diverge. Luther misconstrued thesis one and read it as if it said that the church is a visible gathering. Someone, perhaps Melanchthon, corrected him by saying that the visible church is a gathering. This same unidentified speaker insisted that the assembly of believers is not invisible. Luther, however, had a different starting point and thus did not give up that easily. For him, the church becomes visible in confession of faith according to Rom. 10:10 ("One confesses with the lips and so is saved"). For Luther, the church is incarnate. Striking a similar theme to what he had argued with Ambrose Catharinus twenty years earlier, he put it this way.

> It is necessary that the church be wrapped in flesh, but it is not flesh nor does it live according to the flesh. So also, the church exists in the world, but it is itself not the world nor does it live according to the world. It is in a person, and yet it is not a person or according to a person. Therefore, insofar as the church is in the flesh, in the world, and in a person, it is visible, namely, from its confession [of faith].[53]

A Church of Inclusion under the Gospel

A third issue, whether the papists are in the church, revealed a surprising, truly ecumenical shift on Luther's part. The argument ran: Because the papists did not have the forgiveness of sin (having obscured it with works), they could not be in the church. One might imagine that Luther would have agreed with such an attack on his archenemies. He did not. In fact, he used the notion of the marks of the church to prove that the church has always existed even within the papacy. Lutherans have not always appeared as ecumenical as their founder was. Some cannot even see their way clear to pray publicly with other Christians at a time of national crisis. Luther's approach, however, explains why, for later Lutherans, the truly crucial passages in any ecumenical agreement are those dealing with the actual teaching. For, as long as the external marks of church remain, there is church.

> The church has always existed although not visibly. So, where have the external marks *(notae)* remained? In the church of the papists there remain the true Scripture and that itself preserved by the miraculous counsel of God. Baptism, the Sacrament of the Altar and absolution remain, preserved by divine miracle. Likewise, many died in the true faith and hated the papists and monks. For example, my own father, when he was near death and the monks wanted to harass him with their good works, *he didn't want to hear anything about that stuff* but wanted to die in the faith of our Lord Jesus Christ. He greatly hated the papists. Again, many good monks lived, such as Bernard and Bonaventure, who have been saved. However, they did not have things so clearly as we do now. Likewise, many young children are saved, whom God has freed. The external signs were there. They had absolution of the keys, baptism (although later it was distorted), the text of the Scripture (but later with the great profanation of the bishops).[54]

We sometimes forget that the reformers' own parents lived and sometimes even died in the old church. Here Luther included in the true church not only his own father but also some well-known Christians of the Middle Ages (Bernard and Bonaventure) and even children. For him, church was less an institution and more an event. It occurred precisely where God's word and faith collided. There, faith may grow no matter who plants the message or tends to the seedlings. Or, to use another Pauline metaphor, building on the foundation, Jesus Christ, may take the form of precious stones and gold or straw. The building belongs to God. This ecumenical perspective allowed Luther to accept even that poorest of all Christian theologians, James, into the canon. Thus, we should translate his judgment on James, *ein recht strohernde Epistel,* as "an epistle really building with straw [on the one foundation, Christ]."

With Luther's ecumenical ecclesiology, one never has to reach the absurd point of excluding Roman Christians ipso facto from the church and thus from salvation. Luther's approach stands in judgment over the desperate attempt in *Dominus Jesus* to maintain Roman hegemony. That recent papal encyclical shows just how bankrupt a power-based (as opposed to a gospel-based) ecclesiology really is and how great a challenge the contemporary ecumenical movement (including the Vatican II council) poses to such an approach. They cannot, dare not, judge other Christian churches on the basis of their proclamation of the gospel but only on the basis of communion with Rome. There is, finally, only one mark of the church for them: communion with Rome alone. All else is secondary. That is why the joint declaration on the doctrine of justification—for all of its glaring flaws of theology but with its explicit rejection of any ecclesiological preconditions—may have posed more of a threat to Rome's ecclesiology than to Wittenberg's theology.

The Ministry and the Authority of Apostolic Succession
Here, with remarkable applicability to the current situation, early Lutherans were debating the question of apostolic succession. At every stage, however, their answers differ from the present debate and provide guidelines for a truly evangelical ecclesiology, shorn of any doses of nineteenth-century romanticizing of bishops on the one side or congregational pietism on the other.

The debate began, as did all parts of academic disputations, by posing the alternative. "Where there is church, there is the [public] ministry. However, the ministry requires ordinary succession. Therefore, etc." The questioner was asking whether "ordinary succession," that is, ordination by means of bishops in communion with Rome, was necessary.

Macchabäus provided an initial answer. The ministry requires succession, though not of the kind that they had under the papacy. It does not require succession bound to a particular place. He also provided the standard papal argument: "Peter had his see at Rome. We

Roman bishops are the successors of Peter. Therefore we hold the see at Rome." Macchabäus insisted that the conclusion is incorrect.

Luther, however, went much further than his student had. In the theological freedom typical of Wittenberg's most famous reformer, Luther began not by attacking Rome but by examining Wittenberg.

> Succession is bound to the gospel. If the bishop, successor to Pomerania [Bugenhagen] in this church were to teach the devil, I ought not obey him because *it says*, "Flee false prophets." According to this text, *a person should observe where the word is*. Not because he succeeds [a bishop], but because he walks in his footsteps. Where the word is, there is the church. *That is correct.* We ought not argue this way: The gospel was in Wittenberg a few years ago, therefore now, too, it is there. A bishop must be believed not because he succeeded the bishop of that place but because he teaches the gospel. *The gospel should be the succession.*[55]

A different version of the same debate puts it this way:

> In the church, the gospel ought to be the succession. Thus, those who succeed true bishops in ministry but do not teach what their predecessors taught are not bishops but heretics and, as Paul says [Gal. 1:9], must be held anathema, because they are not bound to a place but to the gospel. Whoever teaches as their predecessors must be obeyed; if they teach less than their predecessors, like heretics, they must be opposed.[56]

As Luther had throughout the twenty-six-year debate over ecclesiology, he used Gal. 1:9, rejected any attempt to tie authority to a place or person, and placed the gospel in the center. However, what strikes the reader is that, unlike Reformed and later pietistic rejections of episcopacy per se, Luther insisted that Christians owe obedience to bishops who succeeded their predecessors by being true to the gospel.

Proof for the Evangelical Origin of the "Marks" of the Church
In the context of this debate, Bugenhagen himself, professor at the university and chief pastor and bishop of Wittenberg, reflected an argument of the opponents regarding the "marks" of the church itself.

The very way he posed the objection demonstrated that even the Wittenbergers realized that the terminology was new.

> Christ does not describe these marks of the church proposed by you. Nor does he say, "You must be Christians because you have the Gospel and sacraments." Besides, the papists do not acknowledge us as Christians on account of these marks. But Christ says, "In this all will know that you are my disciples, if you remain in love." [John 13:35] Therefore, the mark of the church is love.[57]

This indicated just how novel the marks of the church, as Luther defined them, really were. The respondent, probably Macchabäus, pointed to Matt. 28:19 and argued that love is comprehended in the sacraments themselves.

Arguments against Claims of Ordinary Succession
A little later in the discussion, a young student at the urging of Bugenhagen posed the following dilemma. Bishops attain ordinary succession not by civil election but through a call and ecclesiastical election. Thus, they have ordinary succession from the time of the apostles and must, therefore, be obeyed according to Luke 10:26 ("Whoever hears you, hears me") because they are successors to the apostles. It appears that Luther responded, in the first instance, by distinguishing human call from the call of the Holy Spirit. How can one determine that they have no call through the Holy Spirit? "Because they do not care for souls but instead seek dignity and wealth."[58] This defined clearly the evangelical episcopate: a ministry of care for souls, congregations, and pastors.

The Word Makes the Ministry
Veit Winsheim, a professor of medicine at Wittenberg, raised the following objection. "The church is bound to the ministry of the word (according to Paul in Eph. 4:11f.). Therefore, it is impossible that all ministers everywhere err. As a consequence, it is necessary that in the church there is an order in which the promise of truth resides."[59] This was no small argument, and it is still a favorite objection by Roman Catholics to what they perceive as the chaos of Protestantism.

Luther's answer again puts the lie to the kind of democratized view of ministry rampant in today's church while, at the same time, not capitulating to the papalists.

> It is true. The church is bound to the ministry, to the gospel, but not to the ministers. Those ministers are a gift given by God to the church; they are not the head of the church. Knowledge of the truth pertains to the ministers. Ministry of the word makes ministers; ministers do not make the ministry of the word. The word does it.[60]

Luther's Sermon on the Baptism of Jesus (13 January 1544)[61]

How did this play in Peoria? Did these critical but technical arguments have any place in parish life? Luther's sermon on the baptism of Jesus, preached on the first Sunday after the Epiphany in 1544 demonstrates at least one way in which they mattered. An analysis of this sermon constitutes the final section of this chapter.[62]

Theology of the Cross[63]

First, ecclesiology has to do with the theology of the cross, which Luther defined as the way God goes about revealing himself—not only on the cross but in every aspect of the scriptural witness. The scandal of the cross and the paradox of the incarnation elucidate the theology of the cross at every turn. It is, to quote Luther, the revelation of God *sub contrario specie,* that is, under the appearance of the opposite or, in modern parlance, in the last place human beings would reasonably think to look. In this case, if reason comes in and tries to judge the presence of the Trinity at Jesus' baptism, it is flummoxed. Or in Luther's pithy phrase: "Mathematics won't work here." What comfort that remains for those who live in an age that thinks it has everything figured out!

Jesus' Baptism Opens Heaven Once and for All[64]

One of the greatest problems with scripture and preaching in the ELCA and other churches today is that everyone thinks the Bible is a closed book. Some think that the only way to understand the text is to engage in "highfalutin'" criticism—as if knowing the historical or literary details of every text makes a sermon. Others, leaving the text far behind, regale their listeners with interesting stories but never lead them into the text itself. How sad when a preacher leaves a parable of Jesus to tell a story of his or her own devising, as if Jesus' story wasn't good enough or clear enough. The genius of Luther's preaching is that he led his hearers into the text and let the story itself create more than enough drama and excitement. He did this with a kind of exegetical imagination that remained faithful to the historical and literary details of a text by opening the heart of scripture to the hearer.

In this case, he noticed that the heavens opened when Jesus was baptized. He then brought that fact crashing into the listeners' present by insisting that those same heavens were not shut again. They were still open! That meant that church, as an event, happens every time the preacher simply tells the truth ("The heavens are still opened") and points to places where that opening occurs. Where? Where, indeed! In the marks of the church! A preacher crawls into the pulpit on Sunday morning and has something to say only by virtue of the fact that at Jesus' baptism the heavens were opened! However, because the heavens are open, it is not the preacher's voice but Christ's that sounds. What comfort this is for the church! No wonder this is the gate of heaven!

The Trinity's Presence in the Face of Persecution[65]

For Luther, preaching was not a matter of knitting pious platitudes together. It was a matter of telling the truth of God *in the face of* the truth of human existence. God's truth? The Trinity surrounds believers in the church! The human truth? Believers are under attack! What a powerful line Luther borrowed from Zechariah! The "apple of the eye" is reflection of a person's face in the eye of another. It can only be seen when two people stand closely enough together to see that reflection in the pupil. Believers are so intimately associated with the Trinity that to touch them is to touch the apple of God's eye! What comfort to know God will never abandon them—no matter how badly things go!

God's Two Hands[66]

At the time this sermon was preached, Luther was locked in a struggle with the law faculty at the University of Wittenberg. He had accused them of confusing the law in this world with the Christian law of love. As he had throughout his career, Luther insisted that one must distinguish between the needs and wants of this world and the good news of the world to come.

To be sure, justice in this world is important. However, when pastors visit someone in distress, they must speak about something more than that! I once heard that each year 50 percent of adult Americans are touched with the loss of a loved one or friend. Whether this is true or not, there is every reason for preachers to speak of what God in Christ gives to humanity: forgiveness of sin, life, and salvation. To those who object that this is pie in the sky, there are two responses: "Don't you like pie?" and "The sky is falling!" In any case, justice is not established among Christians by merely railing at them with the law. Christian preachers proclaim heavenly treasure, which has the immediate benefit of putting what Luther called "trashy, earthly goods" in proper perspective. For Luther, this also put an end to the papal pretense of being the judge of kings or presidents.

Pastors Are Lords over the Devil[67]

Pastors and preachers are engaged in a spiritual warfare, no less risky than the political responsibility of a president or prime minister. Because pastors think so little of the devil, they do not realize what power they have. Some time during her battle with terminal cancer, my wife was stricken by depression—the sort that often arose with her kind of disease. The pastor came to the house that afternoon and said two things that broke the bonds of that spiritual prison. "Go ahead and be depressed," he said. "We, your fellow believers, will carry you now." No governmental official, no doctor, not even a psychiatrist, could say such powerful words.

There is an authority that pastors possess by virtue of their office. They can tell the devil to go to hell, and to hell he must go. When they say the word, that is it. It is all over but the shouting! Pastors, and all Christians for that matter, simply traffic in the marks of the church. The wonder of it is hard to comprehend! When bishops say to someone (using Luther's words in this sermon), "You shall be a priest," it happens—not by their power and authority but by the power and authority of Christ who has created the office of bishop and placed them in it. Lutherans and other Christians can argue all they want about whether a bishop absolutely has to be present at an ordination. But if I were a bishop, I wouldn't miss an ordination for the world! God gives bishops the hand and mouth so that, "when we impose our hands, this is as valid as if God himself did it." Which bishop would want to miss that? Who of us would want to leave them out?

Common Priesthood of All Believers[68]

One of the foolish mistakes some make in the church today is to drive a wedge between the public office of the ministry and what is often called the priesthood of all believers. (Actually, a better translation of Luther's *das allgemeine Priestertum aller Gläubigen* would be "common priesthood of all believers.") First, there is never any sense in which Luther first supports the general priesthood and then, because of the Anabaptists or the Peasants' War or some such thing, becomes reactionary and flips back to support the public office of ministry. This pietistic sleight-of-hand has no basis in fact.[69] Luther always had the highest regard for the public office of ministry. The common priesthood was for him not something a single person exercised publicly.[70] It is rather what Christians hold in common. It is what happens to us because Christ is our Great High Priest who offered himself for us once for all.

In an emergency, when there is no one else around, then anyone must step in and fill that public office, by virtue of his or her baptismal ordination. However, this is not an exercise of the common priesthood of all but specifically of the public office of ministry. For Luther, when the conscience is afflicted, it must have a word from God. In his eyes, the heavens are open! The Father's voice still sounds! The Holy Spirit hovers over the scene. The Son is baptized. In an emergency, the gospel waits for no one. The public office it creates demands to be filled. Many denominations, including the ELCA, are now entering an emergency in the church where many smaller rural and urban churches have no one to serve them regularly. Given the emergency, what can a bishop do but grab a child, a man, or woman and get the office filled? Even if the Lutheran Church–Missouri Synod will not ordain women on the basis of equality, given their need, they should be more than willing to allow it in the emergency situation we now face. The gospel, like a funeral procession in a city, runs all the red lights in order to get where it is going, breaking even those rules that determine who can or cannot preach, teach, or administer the sacraments.

Luther reflected at length on the spiritual power possessed in the office. Pastors sit in "spiritual places" according to Ephesians. And, to Luther, that meant that we rule like kings and queens, not against the political enemies of the Democrats or Republicans, but against the devil himself. By virtue of the common priesthood, Christians do this for one another all the time in their daily life. By virtue of the public office, pastors, teachers, and bishops do this in and for the church. And when they fail to show up, then God will raise up a Deborah or, if that is what it takes, Balaam's ass. Now that is a comfort!

Pastors Are Powerful Dirt Bags[71]

Luther calls the human being, himself, a sack of maggots or maggot feed, what in the 1970s Americans called dirt bags, but for which the proper term is now scum bags. Yet we judge angels! We can say to every evil force that attacks us, "Leave my soul in peace, for Christ has redeemed it. Take that, Satan!" This paradox stands at the heart of all apostolic and historical succession in the public office of ministry. Succession must rest not in human hands but in Christ's wounded hands. His coming into the flesh meant for Luther that God continues to use flesh—human tongues and hands—to do his work on earth. It must tick the devil off! Except, of course, most Christian pastors do not believe it! Instead, they live and work as teachers, pastors, and bishops of the church as if there were no God at all, or at least not a God who would use human voice and hands to build the church. But what a comfort if one dared believe it!

Pastors Are Sinners[72]

Nowadays, most people know this, at least on a theoretical level. However, the comfort and consolation here consists of the fact that God actually uses sinners to bring in God's rule. Sinner and maggot fodder though they are! Who would have thought! So why do pastors and bishops so often bore people with silly stories in their sermons when they can preach this miracle of God and raise the dead? God uses sinners to make saints! This provides such comfort for those sinners who are pastors and teachers of the church.

Pastors Struggle[73]

Luther described here the struggle *he himself* had believing all this. Christians treat the baptism of Jesus and the opening of the heavens as if it were a dead story! As if it did not matter! As if preachers could all just yawn and say, "Oh, who cares? I need to increase giving to the synod or put out this or that parish fire today or [fill in the blank]." Pastors, bishops, and congregants alike snore through the gospel and try to think of something relevant to say, when indeed there is nothing more relevant than to say, over and over again, "The heavens are open here at this font, at this table, from this pulpit, in this ordination." Christ has decided, just plum decided to work through this scum bag. What comfort, if only someone believed it!

Grace Alone; Faith Alone[74]

"This is my Son, with whom I am well-pleased." Were ever more gracious words uttered in this world? Luther was simply overwhelmed by the story, for there is nothing else to which faith may cling. There is no other object for faith than this unemployed, soon-to-be crucified carpenter standing dripping wet in the Jordan. And that very baptism makes all baptisms holy and righteous baths, filled with God's gracious promise. Here God clothes the child or adult in silk and calls them children, adopts them into the divine family. Suddenly, nothing else matters. All evil melts in the presence of this Sun of Righteousness. Why would one even dream of doing evil to this gracious God or to one's brothers and sisters in Christ, or to God's creation? For Luther, this is the heart of the church and its marks—the point of it all: comfort that comes from Christ alone. That alone makes all the difference in life. It makes believers church, children of God, and heirs of heaven. Soli Deo gloria!

Now there remains only one question. How might we put this in practice in our church? What might such a church look like in the context of a culture that has a very different view of church? For these matters, Gordon Lathrop will have a word in the sixth chapter.

Chapter 6

The Marks of the Church as a Theme for the Visitation of Parishes

As emphasized above, Lutherans confess that the assembly called "church" has certain recognizable, God-given marks. And Lutherans—together with others whose ecclesiology has been shaped by the idea of the marks—confess that the only God-given authority that bishops[1] have is in the exercise of those marks, in the authority and power employed "by teaching and preaching God's Word and by administering the sacraments."[2] Can we put these two confessed themes together in further reflection on actual care for current congregations?

Bishops and Visitations

Bishops are bishops, precisely as they, in the assembly of the church, exercise and are part of the marks of the church—as they are, in Grundtvig's image, standing at the table and doing so in the service of the gospel. The other tasks and powers they have—given by the ELCA or by a synod or a diocese or by popular expectation or by the civil law, and now also given by ecumenical agreements (as in what the Lambeth Quadrilateral calls "the historic episcopate, locally adapted")—can all be seen as "rites and ceremonies of human institution," on which we have locally, regionally agreed. But like such ceremonies, the evaluation of these tasks and powers must always be based on whether they serve rather than obscure the central matters of the church.

Bishops exercise that preaching, teaching, and sacramental ministry primarily in the midst of the assembly that has called them—

the synod or the diocese—and therefore in the midst of its general assemblies. But they also preach and preside in the midst of its constituent congregations. They visit parishes, congregations, and local assemblies, in the exercise of their ministry. And they have or ought to have no real power there except the power of the word and sacraments. Or, to be realistic, whatever other power is attributed to them needs to be broken to this central work of the gospel. But we have seen that the preaching of the gospel, the celebration of the bath and of the supper, which are full of Christ's presence, the announcement of the forgiveness of sins, public thanksgiving and beseeching, the establishment of ministries, the confession of our own need, and the collections for the wretched of the world—all of which things bishops do in their visitations—are all part of the gospel itself. And these things cannot be without "the Christian holy people" nor can the assembly be "church" without these things.

Therefore, the visitations of bishops and their teaching, rightly, and with the authority of the gospel, should be filled with the encouragement and the support of these things in the midst of each congregation. For congregations are assemblies that constantly need to refind their center, to discover themselves again and again being transformed into church by the action of God in the living marks of the church.

The business of bishops is not to demand or legislate or compel. They probably could not bring off such a style in democratic America if they wanted to. Their task is to teach and encourage. A bishop's task is to be a personal sign of the communion of the churches in the marks of the church, and to do so, in the wonderful ecumenical phrase, by "mutual affirmation and admonition." His or her style may well be to ask questions, engage in dialogue, always open to learning the new ways, in new localities and times, that the central things of the church's life are taking on new cultural clothing.

But the central things still need to be central. The bath, the table, the prayer, the word, the open door (to use the list of the bell)—none of them can be marginalized if we still wish to have a church. All of them require continued renewal. All of them, in the present cultural situation, need the support of teaching and preaching. All of them, in their absence or trivialization, require admonition.

The earliest Lutheran document explicitly and successfully prepared to assist "visitors" in parishes—thus "bishops" or "superintendents"—was the 1528 "Instructions for the Visitors of the Parish
Pastors in Electoral Saxony" or "Visitation Articles," written jointly
by Luther and Melanchthon.[3] This document became a model—
perhaps the most important model—for the ongoing regional
preparation of *Kirchenordnungen* and *kyrkoordningen* in sixteenth- and
seventeenth-century Reformation lands. These church orders, too, are
probably best understood as documents intended to guide a visitation. But then it is fascinating to note that the contents of the first
"Instructions"—as of virtually all other such church orders and visitation articles—are essentially a slightly expanded form of a list of the
marks of the church. A section on doctrine and catechism is intended
to guide the visitors in discussing preaching and teaching the living
word with the pastor. Sections on standards and patterns for the celebration of baptism, Holy Communion, and "the keys" follow. When
the Visitation Articles and later church orders then insert liturgical
material here or later in the document, it is not so much to provide an
actual ritual as to make available evangelical guidance as to the use of
traditional and new material and to make sure that the evangelical
center of worship is not obscured. The nature and the appointment of
ministers is discussed. So are the parish's and the pastor's roles in marriage, in an extension of the concern about teaching and preaching. A
discussion of the ordering of schools has the same concern. And later
documents almost always discuss the "community chest" or the collection for the poor, part of our "open door" or of Nehemiah's "sending
portions for those for whom nothing is prepared." The early Lutheran
business of parish visitation was classically about the refreshment and
encouragement of the marks of the church.

Do we need "visitation articles"? Perhaps. But that is what the lists
of the marks of the church have always been. We simply need to use
them.

In many ways, the ELCA document *The Use of the Means of Grace*[4]
is such a list of the marks of the church turned toward the questions
and dialogue of a parish visitation. The document was sent out in
1997, after a several-year-long, churchwide discussion, as if it were
itself a little visitation in paper form. But its questions and proposals

would be much more alive if they were to come in a person, a person representing the unity of the assemblies and the reality of the whole "assembly of God," a person capable of saying why this continued recovery of the centrality of the marks of the church should be so important. Anciently, even well before the Reformation, that person was the bishop.

We might imagine a refreshment and recovery of the bishop's role in visitation. But, as a sign of the communion of assemblies, we might also imagine a variety of other visitors: persons from neighboring congregations; ecumenical and international visitors; persons sent by the synod or diocese or larger church; professors of theology; and the newest newcomers: people looking for a reliable church. None of these visitors ought have any authority for the reordering of the church except the authority of the gospel. All of these visitors, however, might rightly ask for the clear presence of the marks of the church.

As one thinks about the challenges for a bishop/visitor today, especially two might come to the fore. These are the continual recovery of the central signs of the church's life amid the ecumenical diversity of the present time, and the need for the same recovery among the special characteristics of American "evangelical" religious life. In what follows, these two issues will be briefly addressed, in the hope of beginning to sort out various tools or questions that may be useful in actual parish visitation.

Visitation in an Ecumenical Age

For the first concern, a visitor might wisely look at a recent document from the Faith and Order Commission of the World Council of Churches. This document may, in part, be able to function for us like a kind of Instruction for Visitors. The document, drafted in 1994 in Ditchingham, England, and called "Towards Koinonia in Worship," could provide us with a number of questions for affirmation and admonition as we attend together to the life of our congregations. Here is an extensive excerpt.[5] Watch for the marks of the church:

1. . . . Blessed be God's great love which has already given us the holy koinonia for which we pray through the one baptism into Christ Jesus, which continually founds and forms all the churches. Beyond our expectation, God has given us that *koinonia* as we all, together, being "buried with Christ by baptism into death," are raised with him day after day "by the glory of the Father, so we too might walk in newness of life" (Rom. 6:4). That *koinonia* has been given us in the common life of the believing community, which is empowered with many gifts by the Holy Spirit, which eats and drinks the "holy communion" of Christ, and which shows forth a foretaste of the communion of the whole creation with God, a foretaste of all peoples reconciled to God and to each other through the cross and resurrection of Jesus Christ. The gift we have received is our calling and task. The koinonia we seek between and within the churches is a koinonia in and through Jesus Christ. It is a participation in the grace and eternal life of God for the sake of the life and salvation of the world. "God is faithful, by whom you were called into the fellowship of his Son, Jesus Christ our Lord" (1 Cor. 1:9).

2. This crucified and risen Christ, the ground and source and center of our koinonia, is alive today in our midst. Koinonia is found in the scriptures opened to speak of him to our burning hearts (Luke 24:13-32), in the broken bread and cup of blessing which are a participation in the body and blood of Christ (1 Cor. 10:16), and in the one Spirit in which "we were all baptized into one body" of Christ (1 Cor. 12:13). Word and sacraments, signs of the presence of Christ, are set forth in the midst of a participating assembly of people who are gathered by the Spirit, blessed with many different gifts, and sent to bear witness with their lives to the same love and mercy of God for all the world which has been shown forth in their assembly.

3. Through the coming of the Spirit, Christian worship is thus a continual meeting with Christ, so that we might be gathered into the grace and life of God. Many different Christian traditions enrich us as we think of the meaning of this encounter: It is a speaking of the gospel of Christ so that we might come to faith. It is grace flowing from the sacrifice of

Christ. It is the beginning of the transfiguration of all things in
the Spirit of Christ. It is a gift and call for personal holiness
according to the measure of Christ. It is the visible manifestation of the incarnation of Christ so that we might be formed in
incarnational living amid the "sacrament of the world." It is
beholding Christ in the gathering so that we might be able to
behold him and love him among the marginalized, outcast and
disfigured ones of the world. It is participation in the Spirit-led
meeting as "baptism" and in every shared meal as the "Lord's
Supper." It is praise and thanksgiving to the Father through
Christ in the unity of the Spirit. But all these understandings
depend upon Christian worship being centered in the encounter
with God in Jesus Christ through the power of the Spirit
enlivening the word and the sacraments. And all these understandings presuppose that this encounter occurs in an assembly
which is itself a witness to God's intention with the world and
which forms its participants for a life of witness and service. The
liturgy of Christians occurs in assembly: it also occurs in the
midst of daily life in the world.

4. The pattern of this gathering and sending has come to all
the churches as a common and shared inheritance. That received
pattern resides in the basic outlines of what may be called the
ordo of Christian worship, i.e., the undergirding structure which
is to be perceived in the ordering and scheduling of the most
primary elements of Christian worship. This *ordo*, which is
always marked by pairing and by mutually re-interpretive jux-
tapositions, roots in word and sacrament held together. It is
scripture readings and preaching together, yielding interces-
sions; and, with these, it is *eucharistia* and eating and drinking
together, yielding a collection for the poor and mission in the
world. It is formation in faith and baptizing in water together,
leading to participation in the life of the community. It is ministers and people, enacting these things, together. It is prayers
through the days of the week and the Sunday assembly seen
together; it is observances through the year and the annual common celebration of the *Pascha* together. Such is the inheritance
of all the churches, founded in the New Testament, locally practiced today, and attested to in the ancient sources of both the
Christian East and the Christian West.

5. This pattern of Christian worship, however, is to be spoken of as a gift of God, not as a demand nor as a tool for power over others. Liturgy is deeply malformed, even destroyed, when it occurs by compulsion—either by civil law, by the decisions of governments to impose ritual practice on all people, or by the forceful manipulation of ritual leaders who show little love for the people they are called to serve. At the heart of the worship of Christians stands the crucified Christ, who is one with the little and abused ones of the world. Liturgy done in his name cannot abuse. It must be renewed, rather, by love and invitation and the teaching of its sources and meaning. "And I, when I am lifted up from the earth, will draw all people to myself," says Jesus (John 12:32). The liturgy must *draw* with Christ, not compel.

6. Furthermore, this pattern is to be celebrated as a most profound connection between faith and life, between gospel and creation, between Christ and culture, not as an act of unconnected ritualism nor anxious legalism. Every culture has some form of significant communal assembly, the use of water, speech which is accessible but strongly symbolic, and festive meals. These universal gifts of life, found in every place, have been received as the materials of Christian worship from the beginning. Because of this, we are invited to understand the Christian assembly for worship as a foretaste of the reconciliation of all creation and as a new way to see all the world.

7. But the patterns of word and table, of catechetical formation and baptism, of Sunday and the week, of *Pascha* and the year, and of assembly and ministry around these things—the principal pairs of Christian liturgy—do give us a basis for a mutually encouraging conversation between the churches. Churches may rightly ask each other about the local inculturation of this *ordo*. They may call each other toward a maturation in the use of this pattern or a renewed clarification of its central characteristics or, even, toward a conversion to its use. Stated in their simplest form, these things are the "rule of prayer" in the churches, and we need them for our own faith and life and for a clear witness to Christ in the world. And we need each other to learn anew of the richness of these things. Churches may learn from each other as they seek for local renewal. One community

has treasured preaching, another singing, another silence in the word, another sacramental formation, another the presence of Christ in the transfigured human person and in the witnesses of the faith who surround the assembly, another worship as solidarity with the poor. As churches seek to recover the great pairs of the *ordo,* they will be helped by remembering together with other Christians the particular charisms with which each community has unfolded the patterns of Christian worship, and by a mutual encouragement for each church to explore the particular gifts which it brings to enrich our koinonia in worship.

8. This pattern or *ordo* of Christian worship belongs most properly to each local church, that is, to "all in each place." All the Christians in a given place, gathered in assembly around these great gifts of Christ, are the whole catholic church dwelling in this place. As efforts are made to enable local occasions of ecumenical prayer and as local churches are clarifying the full pattern of Christian worship as the center of their life, a groundwork is being laid for local unity. "Local churches truly united" will be one in faith and witness, and, amid a continuing diversity of expression, one in the practice of the most basic characteristics of the *ordo.* This same pattern or *ordo* of Christian worship is a major basis for the koinonia between local churches, a koinonia spanning both space and time, uniting churches of the New Testament times, of the sweep of Christian history and of the present *oikumene.* Such a koinonia is only enriched by those authentic forms of inculturation which the *ordo* may have taken in each local church, not diminished.

In this document, a short list of the marks is put in local action and then called the *ordo* of Christian worship. Ecumenical assent is given to these central matters as church-making gifts of God. Attention is called to differing ways in which these things are alive and received in differing Christian communities, and these differences are themselves seen as enriching gifts of God. But then the stunning assertion occurs:

> Churches may rightly ask each other about the local inculturation of this ordo. They may call each other toward a maturation in the use of this pattern or a renewed clarification of its central

characteristics or, even, toward a conversion to its use. Stated in their simplest form, these things are the "rule of prayer" in the churches, and we need them for our own faith and life and for a clear witness to Christ in the world.

In the matter of the presence and exercise of the central marks, churches ought not just leave each other alone. Of course, there is legitimate and beautiful diversity. But in regard to the centrality of scripture and the gospel, baptism and the supper, word and sacrament, gathering and sending, churches should call out to each other, admonish each other, encourage each other. The basic work of such "calling out" will be done personally by visitors.

A Brief History of American Frontier Worship

But a second challenge to the marks of the church, perhaps in some places the most serious challenge of all, arises from the American evangelical context in which our congregations are currently working. In order to propose some questions for church visitation, allow me first a digression in liturgical history.

The widely discussed "seeker-targeted service" of present church life has a history we should explore. It is older than the Willow Creek Church and the Community of Joy megachurches. The source of the shape and intention of the seeker service is older even than the Billy Graham revival. It is also older than the work of Robert Schuller at what could be called the first megachurch, the Crystal Cathedral in California, a church that had a strong influence on the development of both Willow Creek and the Community of Joy.[6] And it is older than the patterns used by the youth music groups in which both Bill Hybels and Walt Kallestad, the lead pastors of these communities, had their formative ministerial beginnings.[7] The shape of the worship of the megachurch and of those of our congregations that have sought to follow the megachurches has its roots rather in the patterns behind Billy Graham revivals, Crystal Cathedral services and evangelistic song-fests for young people: in the "camp meeting" of the nineteenth-century American frontier.

The camp meetings themselves had prior models on which they built. Scottish and Scotch-Irish Presbyterians of eighteenth-century North Carolina, Virginia, and Maryland and then, as Europeans migrated further west, of Kentucky and Ohio, remembered the powerful and emotionally moving "communion meetings" of lowland Scotland and of Ulster, and re-enacted them in the new land. These were several-day meetings of preaching and teaching and examination that culminated in the admission to the Lord's Supper of those who had been issued a token by the presiding ministers. Some scholars have argued that the power of these events essentially came to replace the old and beloved pageantry of the mass in the piety of the Scottish farmer, and was intended to do so.[8] In any case, the preaching, examination, and commitment to new life did replace the medieval contrition, confession, and penance that had formerly been used to "fence the table" and that, in many cases, had come to overshadow the communion itself as the central source and pattern for the Christian life.

In the new country, the "communion season" or the "sacrament meeting" of Scottish Presbyterians was now inserted within that eighteenth-century history of revival or "awakening" that had already shaken much of Calvinist America. And the communion meeting was able to provide a massive attraction amid the loneliness and colorlessness of the American frontier.

In August 1801, at Cane Ridge, Kentucky, a sacrament meeting was called—and widely advertised—that soon drew thousands of people and became the symbolic beginning of what is called the "Second Great Awakening." After a few days of preparation, the communion service itself was finally held in the meetinghouse, and to it only a small portion of the total attendance, the token-bearers, was finally admitted. But that service came to be dwarfed by the tent-preaching, the outdoor crowds of strangers that no one screened,[9] the extensive campsites, the entertainments, and the spiritual seizures and displays that surrounded it. Indeed, the "preparation" went on for days after the communion service was over, that service no longer being the goal of the event.

Many subsequent sacrament meetings on the frontier came to be marked by the same displays and the same growing marginalization of the sacrament itself. These gatherings were fun and, for many, emotionally fulfilling. Although orthodox Calvinists often did not know what to make of these events and came to distrust them, more optimistic preachers reveled in the possibilities such crowds gave for "revival preaching" and for conversions. Several new American denominations were born in these events, all of them marked by a desire to recover "New Testament Christianity," and all of them characterized by a kind of "edited" Calvinism. In order to believe in the importance of revival preaching, these Christians needed to dismiss predestination and "limited atonement" (the idea that Christ died only for the elect) and embrace instead the importance of the human free will. Indeed, in revival meetings the accent came to fall on the human decision, on the desire to receive Christ, and on the consequent reformed moral life. Baptism was still practiced, but largely as an indication of commitment on the part of those who had so decided. And the communion was still practiced, but, just as in the middle ages, now made very much less important than the new forms of the process of contrition and penance (*contrition and penance*, note, not *absolution*).

In many ways, however, it was no *denomination* that proceeded from the Second Great Awakening, but a widespread, transdenominational, American movement called "evangelicalism." Evangelicals were (and are) Christians that "required, and made central, an arduous, crisis-like conversion, and that, subsequent to this climactic experience, emphasized a warm, spiritual, affectionate form of religion."[10] In its optimistic erosion of orthodox Calvinism, in its accent on individual spiritual journey and individual decision rather than communal sacrament, and in its pragmatic interest in whatever could encourage that decision, this movement could be regarded as a quintessential version of the American religion.[11]

This movement expressed itself especially in the most pervasive and influential form of Christian worship known in America, the form James F. White calls "frontier worship."[12] In the earliest camp meetings, two parallel processes had existed side-by-side.[13] Communion was there for the traditionalists, the old Christians. It was regulated, of course, by the then widespread interpretation of Paul's

strictures in 1 Corinthians 11, taken to mean that an arduous preparation must precede the sacrament. But for everyone else, the crowds
around the meeting house who would never come inside but who
were themselves struggling to "break through to comfort,"[14] there
were the new techniques of revival. Those techniques were quickly
seen to be *song and display* which then led to *preaching,* which then led
to *conversions.* This emerging *ordo* could be regarded as a new American version of the old Calvinist dependence on the medieval *prone,* the
service of popular preaching and exhortation to penance—rather than
the too inaccessible *mass*—as the source for the shape of worship.[15]

But it remained for the greatest revival preacher of the nineteenth
century, Charles Grandison Finney, to systematize this form and, in a
famous essay of 1835, to endow it with the name "new measures,"[16]
his urging of the use of rousing and emotional song and practical but
moving preaching, among other things, to bring the sinner to conversion. For Finney, God had established no particular system or form
of worship:

> When Jesus Christ was on earth, laboring among his disciples,
> he had nothing to do with forms or measures. And when the
> apostles preached afterwards . . . their commission was, "Go and
> preach the gospel, and disciple all nations." It did not prescribe
> any forms. It did not admit any. No person can pretend to get
> any set of forms or particular directions as to measures, out of
> this commission. Do it—the best way you can—ask wisdom
> from God—use the faculties he has given you— seek the direc-
> tion of the Holy Ghost—go forward and do it. This was their
> commission. And their object was to make known the gospel in
> the *most effectual* way, to make the truth stand out strikingly, so
> as to obtain the attention and secure the obedience of the great-
> est number possible. No person can find any *form* of doing this
> laid down in the Bible.[17]

But Finney could recommend a form that worked in the present time,
and that form looked like the pattern of revival preaching. It is no
surprise, given his critique of historic forms,[18] that he himself would
not see any background to his "new measures" in sacrament meetings

or the medieval prone or the patterns of confession and penance. The resultant *ordo,* so widely found in America and in places influenced by America, from that time until this, was threefold:

- a song service or praise service or "preliminaries," gauged to prepare for the preaching;
- a sermon; and
- a "harvest" of the converts.[19]

This is a pattern most North Americans have seen. The megachurches and the congregations that seek to follow them are massive, contemporary expressions of evangelicalism. It is not only that the seeker services stand in the tradition of the camp meeting, its crowds and its entertainments, but also its opportunities for conversion or for preaching outside anything that looks like a traditional "meetinghouse" or church.[20] It is not only that, like the camp meetings—and like many other evangelicals, with their Wednesday night prayer meetings, down through American history—the megachurches also have special Bible study and sacrament meetings for the believers at other times, with baptisms also as demonstrations of prior decisions. It is not only that the arguments of the leaders sound astonishingly like the arguments of Finney himself. It is also that the megachurches have inherited a modern version of the frontier worship shape, itself the product of "edited" American Calvinism.[21]

Of course, on first glance, it seems like the third part of the frontier *ordo* is missing in the megachurches. But, in fact, this lack is only apparent. Bill Hybels himself often ends his sermon, at the end of the seeker service, with a direct call for decision, even calling for some physical sign, like the raising of hands, to demonstrate that the decision has been made.[22] Even without this gesture, however, one must recall the deep commitment of these evangelicals to a modern, persuasive rhetoric, without the so-easily-suspected high pressure of older revivalists, and full of "safety" for the nonbeliever to meet the "unsafe Christ." And one must remember that these services are situated within a network of processes and procedures to bring the convert into the New Community. At Willow Creek, a seven-step strategy has been followed that leads from seeker-service attendance to the New Community service to participation in a small group to volunteering and tithing.[23] At Community of Joy, the talk has been of a "circle of fulfillment" that leads a convert from membership to maturity to ministry and mission, written covenants of commitment and agreement being signed by the convert at each new stage.[24] Just as contemporary music and drama have replaced the old song service and contemporary, accessible rhetoric has replaced the old sermon, so the small group and the network of volunteers has replaced the old "harvest of converts." But the frontier worship pattern, and its underlying rationale, are still firmly in place. The point is to win individuals through to "comfort," to use the old rhetoric, or to "wholeness," to use the new, by their decision for Christ.

Since, in evangelicalism, the whole purpose of the church is to bring individuals to such a decision, the believers also gather for a service that has the same shape. The repetition of this shape serves the purpose of returning the believer to that pattern wherein he or she was "saved" (brought to wholeness), reinforcing its centrality. But now the pattern is also used to enable the believer to sing out praise to the majesty of God and to learn more about the content of the Bible.

The revitalized use of this frontier pattern in the megachurches and in other congregations influenced by them has been recently discussed in North America as if it were an important new liturgical movement[25] or a new reformation[26] or, even, like Cane Ridge itself, a new Pentecost. One virtue of situating the movement within its American history may be a certain tempering of these claims. But more important help would come from our allowing this history to reintroduce a good and widespread discussion of the old and apparently still unresolved issue that is at the center of the disagreement between the megachurches and classic, ecumenical Christianity: the question of *means,* or what Finney called "measures"—what we are calling the marks of the church. Is the church centered on individuals and their processes of decision-making? Or is it centered on—indeed, created by—certain concrete and communal means that God has given, which bear witness to and give the grace of God, and in which God is present and active? That is the question.

It will not do to answer that the megachurches have sacraments. So did the camp meetings. But the sacraments can be so fenced or so individualized or so transformed into signs of human decision that they yield the ecclesial center of attention to the processes of decision-making, just like medieval penance overwhelmed the communal and sacramental center for which it was originally intended as preparation. Then, from the classic Christian point of view, if decision-making is the central matter, the meeting will not really be around God, no matter how orthodox or trinitarian a theology may be in the mind of the "speaker." For the Triune God comes to expression in a Spirit-gathered assembly that is immersed in the utterly central and utterly indispensable signs of the crucified and risen Christ—in word, table, and bath, side-by-side—and so is brought before the face and into the grace and life of the eternal God. From this understanding, Paul's greeting, "The grace of our Lord Jesus Christ, the love of God, and the communion of the Holy Spirit be with you all" (2 Cor. 13:13), has a concrete liturgical form, in spite of what Charles Finney asserted and many American Christians came to believe. Indeed, it is interesting that in Finney's paraphrase of the Great Commission of Matt. 28:19-20, the very text we have quoted above, Finney leaves both baptism and the triune name unmentioned, while he is eager to invite his readers to whatever works.

Visitation amid the Influences of America's Dominant Religion

It is probably true that the dominant religion of America to this day is a kind of "edited" Calvinism, and that Calvinism had to be so edited in order to exist in volunteerist America. And it is probably true that many residents of America, including Lutherans, Episcopalians, and Roman Catholics, have felt drawn to elements of this tradition in order to feel at home in the land, finding some correspondence between their own traditions of pietism and the American revivalist traditions. Indeed, it is among the pietist strains of American Lutheranism that the frontier pattern of worship has had its greatest Lutheran success.[27] These pietists have frequently forgotten their own formerly fierce commitment to the "means of grace," or, perhaps, have found that their own fierce fencing of the sacrament led to its being fenced out of ordinary life and away from regular worship patterns. In any case, it is certainly true that the evangelical version of the American religious heritage has currently come to a new visibility and centrality in American church life and on the American political scene.[28]

But responsible leaders of the churches in our day need to pay attention to more than media estimations of trends in church life. The media, for example, may well never give much space to the remarkably strong movement among some other American evangelicals for a new recovery of the centrality of the Holy Communion as the principal service of every Sunday.[29] It is as if Cane Ridge were being revisited and the token system reconsidered and rejected. That idea—that recalling and reworking of the heritage of Cane Ridge, that focusing of the crowds and the welcome emotions around the sacrament itself—has important possibilities in Calvinist America. But Calvinism, in whatever altered form, has always had those voices that called it to the sacramental vision of John Calvin and to its own rightful place in catholic Christianity. The nineteenth-century work of John Williamson Nevin,[30] perhaps the wisest voice to be raised in opposition to Finney and the "new measures," has had its brilliant fruition in the excellent American Presbyterian *Book of Common Worship* of 1993.

But for Lutherans the central question of *means* and of the marks of the church is inescapable. Lutherans conceive of the church as formed around the means of grace and impossible without them. Lutherans conceive of faith as enabled by, nourished by, and responding to the means of grace. Lutherans suspect that an over-accent on "my decision" and "my new life" only leads to despair or mutual suspicion or works-righteousness.[31] Lutherans believe in the direct, local accessibility of the grace of God in the proclaimed and sung word, in the celebrated supper, in the announcement of absolution, and in that bath that forms a community around the economy of these concrete means. And Lutherans inherit a pattern of shaping the central service of worship around the *mass* made accessible, not around the *prone* and not around the patterns of *penance*.

It may be unfair to compare the attractions of the camp meeting or of entertainment evangelism to the relics of the Middle Ages and to the indulgence trade. But the comparison is not entirely inaccurate. Relics did draw crowds to wildly popular, advertised phenomena, and they did then place the negotiation for indulgences—a negotiation that an individual could make, taking the place of that other private negotiation of penance—at the center of the religious stage. Martin Luther, in his last sermon three days before his death in 1546, preaching at Eisleben on Matt. 11:25-30, gave Lutherans a set of words that ought not be forgotten. Lutherans should be willing to share these words with their ecumenical partners in the conversation on "measures":[32]

> In times past we would have run to the ends of the world if we had known of a place where we could have heard God speak. But now that we hear this every day in sermons . . . we do not see this happening. You hear at home in your house, father and mother and children sing and speak it; the preacher speaks it in the parish church—you ought to lift up your hands and rejoice that we have been given the honor of hearing God speak to us through the Word. Oh, people say, what is that? After all, there is preaching every day, often many times every day, so that we soon grow weary of it. What do we get out of it? All right, go ahead, dear brother, if you don't want God to speak to you every day at home in your house and in your parish church, then be clever and look for something else: in Trier is our Lord God's coat, in Aachen are Joseph's britches and our blessed Lady's chemise; go there and squander your money, buy indulgence and the pope's secondhand junk; these are valuable things! You have to go far for these things and spend a lot of money; leave house and home empty. But aren't we stupid and crazy, yes, blinded and possessed by the devil? There sits that decoy duck in Rome with his bag of tricks, luring to himself the whole world with its money and goods, and all the while anybody can go to Baptism, the Sacrament, and the preaching-desk! How highly honored and richly blessed we are to know that God speaks with us and feeds us with the Word, gives us Baptism, the keys [absolution], and all the rest! But these barbarous, godless people say: What, baptism? sacrament? God's Word?— Joseph's britches, that's what does it!

"Joseph's britches will do it!" Helped by this wonderful old humor, we must constantly be asking whether it is the enormously attractive, theatrically powerful presence of Joseph's britches—and our own individual religious negotiations somewhere near Joseph's britches—that we are setting out at the heart of our liturgies. Or whether the center is genuinely found in word, sacrament, baptism, and keys.

But this is not to plead for the *status quo*. For many Lutheran congregations could do far more to make sure that word and sacrament are genuinely and accessibly and vigorously at the heart of the meeting. And the megachurches can teach us all many things: the awareness that numerous people today have no understanding at all for the traditions and conventions of Christianity; the honesty that Christianity is genuinely in a marketplace of cultural products; the courage to welcome emotions into the assembly of the people of God; the openness to the stranger; indeed, the open door itself. These traits are all virtues. And those virtues and the sincerity of their proponents, not to mention our common faith in the gospel of Jesus Christ, invite Christians into a continuing dialogue about these issues.

For example, Christians newly fascinated by the worship of the megachurch or other, similarly shaped "alternative worship," might be asked in visitation: Do you really think that Finney was right about Jesus and the apostles, let alone the history of the church? Why do you let yourselves still be determined by these nineteenth-century decisions? Is it not true that Jesus and the early church used baptism and the Supper and the scriptures, not just whatever worked? Where are the scriptures in your meetings, let alone baptism and the Supper? How might your gatherings welcome the stranger and the emotions of the regular attendee to be gathered not around the self and its realization, conversion, decision or growth, but around these concrete gifts of Jesus Christ? How might you revisit Cane Ridge, be done with the new version of the system of penance and open up the meetinghouse and its communion service to everybody? And how might you honor the work of God in baptism—including the baptism of many of those "unchurched" people who are drawn to your seeker services—and not make baptism simply a sign of the decision of the self? In the marketplace of American culture, a marketplace currently and remarkably drawn to such odd phenomena as symbolism and chant, how might you set out the bread of grace rather than the stone of the self?

But there are visitation questions for those of us who think that we love the classic ecumenical patterns of Christian worship as well: Have you fenced the Supper as if it were your own, misreading Paul and forgetting that the "body of Christ" that is to be discerned is the body of the excluded ones? Have you opened your doors at the same time that you have worked on the centrality of the means of grace? Have you worked on the centrality of the means of grace at the same time that you have opened your doors? And have you, too, let your congregations—the very people being gathered and formed by the Holy Spirit—be simply audiences, listening to the performers, unengaged in praying for the needs of others, unengaged in song? Have you served that people, loved them, helped them to be the assembly of God bearing witness, as assembly, in the world?

In these discussions, several old questions will be highlighted again: What is preaching for? How does one lead in an assembly gathered around the means of grace in the life of the Triune God? Now that we know that we have been misreading 1 Corinthians 11, what actual consequences will that knowledge have for church life? Could the meal of Jesus Christ function for some people as a first encounter with the gospel, a way into the economy of Christian life? And how do we make sure that whatever "way in" we practice is personal and loving, but also focused around God and grace and community and service, not just the self?

For all parties to this discussion, the classic *ordo* of the accessible mass—word next to table, scripture next to scripture next to preaching leading to communal prayer leading to the table leading to sending to the poor—and the classic *catechumenate*—personal stories and emotions gathered around the story of the communal scriptures as a way into the water, into the community, and into the community's mission—offer genuine help. We can encourage each other in their recovery and their use. We can welcome, and not fear, genuine diversity in their use. We can discuss and disagree about what it means to exercise them in a market culture.

But one thing is quite clear. Say it directly, simply: Joseph's britches will not do it. The marks of the church, full of God's merciful acting for the life of the world, will.

Dear bishops, dear visitors of congregations—whoever you are—please take courage again in your calling. We need your help.

Perhaps now, reminded by the pungent reflection on Joseph's britches, a last word from Martin Luther on the marks of the church, we might find some renewal of such courage for our time.

Part Two

Mutual Conversation

Chapter 7

The Liturgist Reads
the Historian

One of the medieval wooden churches of Norway, located in a little out-of-the-way village called Uvdal and still in use, has had, since shortly after the Reformation, these words painted on the wall and surrounding the whole assembly: "This is none other than the house of God, and this is the gate of heaven" (Gen. 28:17). The point of the words is that because of God's gift of "baptism, bread and gospel" this assembly is Jacob's Bethel. No need to climb up any ladder. Heaven is still open and God is with us at the foot of the ladder. Here. Now. Not in some pilgrimage spot or wherever they keep Mary's chemise or our former pastor's body. Not in some remembered rally where once I made a decision.

It is a point made, perhaps a little more obscurely, by all the Lutheran congregations in North America that are called "Bethel"— or "Transfiguration" or "Mount Horeb" or "Zion" or a host of other names that point to the presence and appearance and speaking of God. The problem is that the words on the wall or the name of the congregation do not make it so. The marks of the church, God's signs of life, do.

I want to say to you, dear reader—indeed, I want to say to anybody who will listen to me—do you see how Timothy Wengert, in faithful company with Luther and Melanchthon and a whole host of other teachers, is painting those words around any assembly where those signs are alive? And do you see what a gift that is and how much it matters? Here is a richly textured and careful historical account that does not cut history off from us. Here is history that sees our current need, sees the continuity of our need with that of Christians of other times—with that of the old beggar Luther himself—and sees the continuity of the proclamation of God's grace in Christ. And yet, here is history that does not make that vision of continuity into some new fundamentalism, history that also leaves much room to celebrate the differences of the ages and the diversities of our age. The church is not a relic that we may, by hard work, be able to dredge up out of the past. The church is a verb, and it is happening now. But the church is also not a way to organize our own religious feelings of the present, according to our tastes. God is the subject of that verb, and God acts through a few, concrete, real means, means that unite us also with those assemblies of beggars in the past.

The major scholarly contribution that Timothy Wengert has made in these pages is his stunning detective work on the origin of the idea of the marks of the church. This is genuinely new work, and you are reading it here. I freely confess that I was among those who thought—and wrote!—that the idea of the marks of the church was probably at least as old as the Nicene Creed. I gladly stand corrected. There is, for me, both clarity and liberation in that correction. Unity, holiness, apostolicity, and catholicity are indeed characteristics of the church that we can trust only by faith. Baptism, bread, and gospel: these I can see, taste, hear, know. Of course that does not mean that Luther invented the marks! Each of the possible signs or earmarks or colors—both the name and the listings vary, spilling out with the enthusiasm that goes with a newly configured idea— belongs to the gift of Jesus Christ and can be traced in continuity in the churches. But the urgent need to know the church by these marks arose in sixteenth-century controversy and amid the claims of profound pastoral need.

Then it turns out that this idea can be found everywhere in early Reformation teaching and preaching: in confessions and doctoral defenses, in visitation articles and catechisms, in polemical pamphlets and comforting sermons. Indeed, even the catechism as it was reformed in Lutheran hands can be seen as one summary of those marks, a summary very like the ancient Christian way of the catechumens, now put in households and the hands of the people: the preaching of the law, the confession of the gospel, the prayer of Jesus, the bath, the table, and the forgiveness of sins. All of these are assembly events, together meant to bring us to faith in Jesus Christ, together giving birth to the church.

Timothy Wengert helps me to see that this pervasive ecclesiology is not a "partial" or "defective" or "missing" ecclesiology, old canards that even some Lutherans have come to believe of themselves. This ecclesiology, indeed, rolls out "the whole enchilada." This idea about the church can be a proposal to all the churches, rich and full, inviting us to be church in the world today and not just fight about church, and putting our debates about structure very much in a secondary place.

For the urgent pastoral need also belongs to our time. The marks of the church are gifts of God in which God acts. But part of the littleness and vulnerability of these gifts, their appearance *sub contrario,* is that we need to do them. Or we can choose not to do them or to obscure them, marginalize them, forget about them, making ourselves and our own spiritual progress the center of things.

When John Vannorsdall was installed as president of the Lutheran Theological Seminary at Philadelphia almost two decades ago, he spoke of the vocation of the theological seminary to clear out the spring. He remembered the old spring-house that used to stand on many American farms, and the relatively frequent task of clearing out weeds and junk—even the broken-down house itself—so that the water could again flow, clear and accessible. The farmer did not make the water. But the farmer did need to clear out the spring.

Our congregations always need to be clearing out the spring. If the preaching of the gospel makes the church, then the gospel needs to be preached. If the office of ministry is utterly transparent to the means of grace it serves, then that office needs to be exercised in transparency. If baptism and Supper, public thanksgiving and public absolution, and the nontriumphalist solidarity of the assembly with the wretched of the world mark the church so that we can see it, then those things need to occupy the heart of our meetings. We do not make the living water, but we can clear out the spring. Authentic liturgical renewal, in all of the churches, is about that living water flowing, about the happening of these central events, not about some arcane or romantic or tasteful or successful recovery of our own religiousness. A congregation deciding to celebrate the eucharist every Sunday; a pastor deciding to preach faithfully on the lectionary, opening the scriptures to speak of the death and resurrection of Jesus; congregational leaders making of baptism and the way to baptism and the life-long catechumenate of baptism the central events of congregational life; the whole assembly praying in earnest for real needs in the needy world; musicians planning the communal song in such a way that it supports the central marks—these things do not automatically make church, but they sure help to clear out the spring.

I suppose my favorite title for these marks, among the diverse terms Wengert explores, is a title that also recurs in Grundtvig's use: *signs of life*. By this breathing, this heartbeat, you can tell that the body is alive. By this bath and table, prayer and word, you can tell that the church is happening, that you and I are alive together, indeed, that God is alive. As I read it, Timothy Wengert's point is not to argue the finer points of ecclesiology but to urge us to breathe, with the God-given motions of our lungs and heart and with God's own air, not to be so foolish as to suffocate because we refuse the signs of life, liking the plastic bag over our own heads better. *To breathe:* in gospel, sacrament, keys. *To breathe:* in bath and table, prayer and word for all us beggars.

I here thank Tim Wengert for the careful, truthful, yet passionate use of history to serve this breathing.

But, dear reader, I also want to caution you not to misunderstand him on two points. One is the mistake of binding church to place or person. Note that every time our historian discusses this theme, the theology of the cross is never far away. Of course, the gospel occurs in a place—think of that congregation in Uvdal; think of your assembly. The Holy Supper *takes place* in a real *place*. Of course, the gospel occurs among persons, persons bathed in the water of baptism and clothed with the garments of God's mercy. But a certain place—say either Wittenberg or Rome—does not guarantee the gospel. Neither does a certain person. Christ does. Every person and every place is addressed by the gospel, held and cherished by the gospel. That preacher marks the church who preaches and drives Christ, whether it is Judas or

Pilate. That preacher does not mark the church, is not transparent, who just tells his own stories, whether it is Peter or Paul. In such assertions, neither Luther nor Wengert is returning to a Platonist reading of "invisible church," floating above the messy world. If the church is invisible, it is invisible as Christ is, who is hidden in God. Where Jesus Christ is, said old Ignatius of Antioch, there is the catholic church. And, *sub contrario,* that church is always breaking out in the world, where Christ still holds the heaven open, where God stands on the holy ground holding every odd place and every alienated person into hope. So, please, dear reader, do not misuse the idea of "invisible church" to sneak back in some resistance to the concrete means of grace or some standard of our own judgment, secretly administered by you or me, of who is "really" a Christian.

The other caution is about the "word." As Timothy Wengert makes quite clear, Lutherans have sometimes been tempted to think that "word alone" means "book alone" or "doctrine alone" or "didactic sermon alone" or just "pastors talking alone." Bishop Grundtvig can help us here. In his stunning image (see chapter 3), he imagined Jesus speaking through baptism and Supper to awaken the word in the church from the dead: "By awakening his Word from the dead through the means of grace he has awoken the church's hope and confidence which he in the end is himself, the Word of the living God." Sometimes our words in the church do indeed need to be raised from the dead. Interestingly, Grundtvig slightly shifts the rich balance of the marks of the church, as they were alive in Luther's teaching, for a moment giving priority to bath and table, in order to speak clearly the same thing that Luther sought to speak: the living word. The word that is a mark of the church—indeed, the basic mark of the church—will say the same thing that baptism and Supper says, will come to expression best side-by-side with baptism and keys and Supper and prayer, will wash us and feed us and forgive us, like baptism and Supper and keys. Such a word, visible and tangible in these other signs, is finally one Word: Jesus Christ, alive here in the Spirit and spoken by God for the life of the world.

It should be quite clear that this remarkable historian is not inviting us to pretend that we are living in the sixteenth century. Rather, the pastoral needs and polemical edges he explores from that century, have points of contact with our needs. And the simple, lively, short list of the characteristics, marks, *Kennzeichen, notae,* colors, signs of life of the church are indeed gifts to the ages that can set us free to live fully in our own, pluralist, postmodern times. At the heart of otherwise diverse, participating assemblies, these signs of life are not about the pretense of a universal institution nor the imposition of a single way of doing things. They are rather about breathing, living, together, in God's common gift, in what faith says is the one great assembly before God.

Dear Tim: Thank you for painting these old words on our present walls. Because of God's gift of the things we call marks, our own present assembly, wherever it is, is God's house, here, now.

Chapter 8

The Historian Reads the Liturgist

In 1997 the German government struck a two-mark coin in honor of the 500th anniversary of Philip Melanchthon's birth. Graced with a likeness of Wittenberg's second reformer on the obverse, it included in place of milling the following words of Melanchthon, struck into and around the very edge of the coin: "Wir sind zum wechselseitigen Gespräch geboren" (We are born to mutual conversation). This theme of Germany's celebration and Melanchthon's life also aptly describes the work of evangelical theologians—even those who come from the disparate fields of church history and liturgy. Indeed, as I have argued elsewhere, the principle of mutual conversation also marked the relation between Luther and Melanchthon.[1]

To have the opportunity to look over the fence into another scholar's garden is a great honor. Already in the first chapter, Gordon Lathrop puts the reader on notice that it is about assembly, and not just any club or gathering of like-minded individuals, but an assembly gathered by God around word and meal. Yet—and this marks an advantage that the liturgical scholar has over the historian—the grounding of the discussion of marks of the church in the assembly does not revert to a kind of pious romanticism, a nostalgia for the good old days of Ezra, Paul, Justin Martyr, or Martin Luther. Thus the middle of that first chapter includes a brief but important cultural critique or, better, description. "Bowling alone" is simply a quaint example of a much deeper malady that infects out common life: worshiping alone, living alone, dying alone—or rather—doing all these things in virtual, ghostly communities where there is no God and no humanity.

Lathrop also makes clear that catholicity cannot mean universal organization but precisely the local assembly gathered around word and sacraments, the true signs of life for the church. This does not exclude wider gatherings of Christians, but it does mean that unity among Christians finally rests in the very marks that reveal our life to the world. Although he does not mention this, this very interplay between assembly and catholicity stands over against another bugbear with which our culture struggles: globalization in the worst sense of the term. In the end, the scandal of the assembly's particularity, gathered around word and sacrament, clears the way for another, truly catholic vision of the oikoumene.

The appeal that closes this chapter is also the appeal of the entire book: to send Christians back into their assemblies with a renewed sense of whose they are. The gatherings around the word of God—aural and visible—are truly precious, remarkable occurrences each time they take place. When folk gather on Sundays to celebrate the resurrection of the crucified one, they suddenly become caught up in an assembly that stretches from Sinai to the upper room through Wittenberg and Rome to the final gathering of those whose robes are washed white in the blood of the Lamb. How can one fail to encourage all to glimpse just how remarkable these assemblies are?

At precisely the point of this appeal, the witness of church history may "strengthen our weak knees." What Luther and Melanchthon contribute to the discussion of ecclesiology (that is, reflection on assembly) is the largely unspoken leitmotiv of this entire chapter: God is the one who creates assembly, who assembles, who takes those who are "no people" and makes them "God's own." The subject of the verb that is "church" (assembly) is indeed the Triune God who, in Luther's explanation of the Third Article of the Apostles' Creed, "calls, *gathers,* enlightens, and makes holy." For, again in Luther's words but this time from "A Mighty Fortress," "Did we in our own strength confide, our striving would be losing." Thus, any admonition to cherish the assembly must always come with the confession that the assembly is already cherished in and by God.

At the same time, this means that recognition of the miraculous, God-given nature of the assembly occurs only by faith alone. It is true: the visible marks of such an assembly are there for all to see, but they are always marked by cross and suffering *(Anfechtung)*. Thus, in the midst of all the things that threaten to wreck this very assembly, only by faith "steals on the ear the distant triumph song." Thus, there is a decided tone proclaiming God's grace and mercy throughout this book but especially in its first chapter, so that "hearts are brave again and arms are strong." It is in the light of faith that the admonition becomes what it most truly is: invitation, indeed eschatological invitation.

In Lathrop's second contribution (the third chapter in this book), there is a phrase that catches the eye: "the absence of triumphalism in worship." For reasons that only a computer programmer would know, the word is not in the standard dictionary and therefore gets underlined in red on my computer screen. Perhaps, in the world of computer giants, the word, like Rumpelstiltskin's name, dare not be spoken. As Lathrop makes clear, however, the best inoculation against such triumphalism may well be the marks of the church.

Here, again, he demonstrates the advantages of a liturgical theologian over (at least) this church historian. He can easily jump from Luther to the Augustana to Sjaeland to Grundtvig to Midwestern bells and draw them together as a coherent witness. Marks of the church are not just historical niceties preserved in musty creedal statements. They truly are signs of life and movement and music. In one sense, because these very signs are marked by the cross and not by glory, their existence may seem ephemeral—like the pealing of the bells calling me to worship this very Sunday.[2] Yet in these unlikely places—a tract by Luther, a hymn by Grundtvig, a picture by some anonymous Dane, and a bell destroyed by fire—we catch a glimpse of God's living assembly.

The "every seeking soul" of the bell's inscription might, in the hands of someone less skilled than Lathrop, also give an opening to triumphalism. As if the point were to admonish the soul to seek! But here the seeker is not the one full of his or her culture and convinced of his or her power to decide. Instead, the seeker is the empty one, driven by the law into the arms of Christ, into the waters that join us to Christ's death and resurrection, into the participation of his body and blood, into hunger for the word of life, and finally into the lap of "our Father," who, in the familiar words of Luther's explanation to the Lord's Prayer, would "entice us . . . to come."[3] The bell does nothing more (or less) than repeat Philip's famous words to a skeptical Nathanael: "Come and see!"

Finally, in this chapter, Lathrop adds an important twist of his own, something that one can only see in the varied dress and sex and age of the worshipers depicted in the Danish altarpiece. The marks of the church look outward. Already, Luther's addition of prayer points in that direction, as does the central place of the cross. But it was only in the work of reformers like Grundtvig that the full potential of this outward-looking assembly came to be plumbed. What "breaks down the dividing wall" (Eph. 2:14) is Christ and his death, not simply our own schemes for outreach or mission. The final paradox of the marks of the church is this. The one to whom they point, the one in the center of the assembly—Christ crucified and risen—is the very one who suffered outside the city gate. This is the heart of Christ's "otherness," in which all the marks of the church share. It is no accident that Luther sometimes ended his sermons with pleas to contribute to the community chest. Helping one's neighbor, the other, is where the church's marks—the marks of the crucified—lead us.

In Lathrop's final contribution, chapter 6, we first encounter the evangelical bishop, what Luther termed a true visitor. Here we see, in the first instance, a re-envisioning of the *evangelical* office of bishop—grounded in the very marks through which God creates church and for which God instituted the office of pastor and bishop. Two historical notes about those visitation articles of 1528 come to mind.[4] First, the English translation of the German title obscures the very thing Lathrop emphasizes most clearly. It is not Instructions *for* the Visitors—Melanchthon, Luther, and John Bugenhagen (Wittenberg's pastor) were both the visitors and the authors of the document. It is rather *Instructions by the Visitors for the Parish Pastors in Electoral Saxony*. This underscores both the authority of the visitors and their task: affirmation and admonition concerning the marks of the church.

The second point is even more telling. When visitation teams went forth through Saxony in 1527–1529, they had four members:

two from the Saxon elector's court, one law professor from the University of Wittenberg, and a theologian—for the most part, Philip Melanchthon, who had been elected by the theological faculty at Luther's insistence. In the emergency of the Reformation with the collapse of episcopal authority, the prince had taken upon himself to embark on a visitation—Luther likened it to Constantine's calling the Council of Nicea. The power of the court and its lawyers was needed especially to bring the churches' financial house in order. (The visitors discovered pastors unpaid for two years!) But, in contrast to financial and administrative questions, under whose authority would the Visitation Articles themselves stand? Surely not the elector's or the court's, but then whose? The answer is on the cover of the *Instructions by the Visitors*. At the top is depicted the Trinity, at the bottom the birth of Christ, and on each side stand the coat-of-arms of the most important ecclesial visitors: Martin Luther's rose and Philip Melanchthon's serpent on a pole (cf. John 3:15). When the same *Instructions* were republished in 1538, five such insignia surrounded Christ bearing a lamb on his shoulders. They represented the five theologians on Wittenberg's faculty: Justus Jonas, John Bugenhagen, Caspar Cruciger Sr., Luther, and Melanchthon. The face-to-face quality of the visits, for which Lathrop appeals in his discussion of how we might employ "The Use of the Means of Grace," is given visual weight in these emblems.

Besides focusing on the visitors of today's churches and making a plea for the revitalization of such visits in parish life, Gordon Lathrop also brings the wider church into the conversation, lest the very Lutheran nature of the discussion here give rise to a particularly virulent form of Lutheran triumphalism. The important witness of Ditchingham points to the very ecumenical nature of the church's marks and also proves the continuing importance of the slogan for Melanchthon's year: We *are*—all of us—as Christians born to mutual conversation, affirmation, and admonition. Sometimes ecumenical discussions may seem foreign to church life and, despite their formulators' best intentions, may even become church-dividing. Here, however, the Lutheran discovers the very opposite—a wholly ecumenical convergence, which, at the same time, is rooted in the very "signs of life" and "characteristic markings" of the church.

On the other hand, Lathrop's final section of this chapter brings into focus just how difficult it may be for some to hear and experience the joy of these marks that stand at the center of the church's life and, indeed, give the church life. Current struggles in North American church life are not so much over traditional or contemporary worship styles; they are rather over the very marks of the church. For the opposite of these marks is always and only the self and its decisions. Any time human decisions and works become the center of the assembly or any time we use our works to fence the marks of the church from the people, then there is only death—for that is what we bring to Christ's table, with or without Joseph's breeches.

In this regard, Lutherans have something quite remarkable to offer as a replacement both for all the appeals to choose Christ or decide for Jesus and for all of the fences we construct to protect the church's marks. Luther's explanation to the Third Article of the creed says it best.

> I believe that by my own understanding or strength I cannot believe in Jesus Christ my LORD or come to him, but instead the Holy Spirit has called me through the gospel, enlightened me with his gifts, made me holy and kept me in the true faith, just as he calls, gathers, enlightens, and makes holy the whole Christian church on earth and keeps it with Jesus Christ in the one common, true faith. Daily in this Christian church the Holy Spirit abundantly forgives all sins—mine and those of all believers. On the Last Day the Holy Spirit will raise me and all the dead and will give to me and all believers in Christ eternal life. This is most certainly true.[5]

Here the marks of the church, described by a list of verbs, find their true subject, the Holy Spirit, who uses them to make believers, gather believers, and, finally, raise believers to eternal life. That finally is the mutual, independent discovery to which we both have come: that God *marks* the assembly with Word and Sacrament, with prayer and proclamation (under the cross), and *sends* us into the world marked with those very gifts for all. Then there is no more room for boasting or asking what "works"—for the working and the glory belong to God alone.

The Promotion Disputation of Johann Macchabäus of Scotland

Portions of Philip Melanchthon's Theses

1. [146] The visible church is an assembly of saints, in which many hypocrites are mixed, who nevertheless agree concerning true doctrine and have external signs, profession of pure teaching of the gospel and the legitimate use of sacraments.

2. I call "saints" in this life those who believe in the gospel and are reborn through the Holy Spirit, who truly pray to God by trusting in the mediator, and have an inchoate obedience.

3. The church is bound to the gospel according to the voice of the eternal Father concerning the Son ("Listen to him"); it is not bound to bishops or to the ordinary succession of bishops.

4. When bishops oppose the gospel, we are forced by divine command to leave them as "anathema" according to the saying of Paul [Gal. 1:8]: "Whoever teaches another [147] gospel, let that one be anathema." That is, let the one cursed by divine judgment be counted as excluded from the church and rejected, one to be avoided lest the contagion pollute others, as in Psalm [109:18f.]: "He put on a curse as clothing."

5. Human governments are bound to a certain succession. They have kings and power to interpret their laws; they have distinctions among persons. Kings and dukes have some glory, that is, power, wealth, and worthiness of their deeds; e.g., Alexander the Great and Scipio did great deeds.

6. The church is not such a political entity but a dispersed body, which is found throughout the entire earth without a head, without power, without human glory. That is, without riches and without grades of human dignity.

7. But they have a head, Christ, who is present with his members and rules and defends them. It has glory as well, because it knows and celebrates God. Moreover, it does great deeds, as Elijah, Elisha, Paul, and other godly did, who prosecuted a bitter war against the devil, one that affords no truce, so that many were freed from eternal death.

8. In the church, there must be judgments, and [in the church] there is the gift of interpreting scripture. This is the "regal and praetorian" power of interpreting scripture. That is, because of the authority of order, it is necessary to obey such a person.

9. However, it is clear that the bishops of this day are idolaters and enemies of the gospel, because they defend much idolmania and many errors that fight perniciously against the gospel.

Theses 10-18 described this idolmania as (10) invocation of the dead; (11) the papist mass; (12) sacrifice of the mass; (13) applying mass to others; (14) applying the mass to the dead; (15) this use means it is not a true sacrament; (16) monastic life merits forgiveness; (17) prohibition of marriage; (18) doctrine of justification. Theses 19-23 described the evangelical understanding of justification and penance. Thesis 24 attacked satisfaction, and thesis 25 concluded that there can be no friendship with the papists.

Portions of the Disputation

[160]: XI. To obey those set above you [Heb. 13:17] is godly and holy. Bishops are set above us, therefore to obey bishops is a godly and holy work.

Response of Martin Luther: This text of the epistle to Hebrews does not conflict with our position as long as it is properly understood. For he adds, "To obey those placed above you, namely, those who are vigilant in caring for souls," as if providing rationale for

[161] them, "is a godly and holy work." However, in this way I accept the major premise but deny the minor. For our bishops are not vigilant for us but are rather pernicious wolves attacking the consciences of souls. They are vigilant instead that souls may perish rather than be saved. They do not exercise care of souls.

XII. The gathering of those who believe is not visible. The church is a gathering of believers. Therefore, the church is not visible.

The solution of Martin Luther: On account of [its] confession [of faith] the gathering of the church is visible. "By the mouth confession is made for salvation" [Rom. 10:10].

Another response [Melanchthon?]: We have made the word "visible" modify the subject, you understand it to modify the predicate. We say, "The visible church is a gathering," not "The church is a visible gathering." But I deny the major in this syllogism, where although it is among you on the inside (that is, we cannot discern faith), nevertheless we may see those who believe.

What follows is from Dr. Martin Luther: From confession the church is recognized, according to the saying of Paul cited above [Rom. 10:10], "For one believes with the heart and so is justified, and one confesses with the mouth and so is saved." It is necessary that the church be wrapped in flesh, but it is not flesh nor does it live according to the flesh. So also, the church exists in the world, but it is itself not the world nor does it live according to the world. It is in a person, and yet it is not a person or according to a person. Therefore, insofar as the church is in the flesh, in the world, and in a person, it is visible, namely, from its confession [of faith].

[162] [XII] Against these things [this is only in one manuscript]: Articles of faith are not seen. "I believe in the church" is an article of faith. Therefore, the church is not visible.

Response: There are four terms. For the article of faith is not seen, that is, those propositions are not seen, but the scope or subject is seen. You do not see this proposition, 'I believe that God has created heaven and earth,' but nevertheless I see the subject, heaven and earth.

[167] [XIX: from ms. A, against thesis one]: Since the church of the papists did not have forgiveness of sins, then it was not the church, because outside the church there is no remission of sins.

Response of Martin Luther: The church has always existed, although not visibly. So, where have the external marks [*notae*] remained? In the church of the papists there remain the true scripture and that itself preserved by the miraculous counsel of God. Baptism, the Sacrament of the Altar, and absolution [168] remain, preserved by divine miracle. Likewise, many died in the true faith and hated the papists and monks. For example, my own father, when he was near death and the monks wanted to harass him with their good works [German], he didn't want to hear anything about that stuff [Latin] but wanted to die in the faith of our Lord Jesus Christ. He greatly hated the papists. Again, many good monks lived, such as Bernard and Bonaventure, who have been saved. However, they did not have things so clearly as we do now. Likewise, many young children are saved, whom God has freed. The external signs were there. They had absolution of the keys, baptism (although later it was distorted), the text of the scripture (but later with the great profanation of the bishops).

[167] XIX [the same arguments from ms. B]: Forgiveness of sins is not outside the true church. In the papistic church there was no forgiveness of sins. Therefore, there was then at that time no true church.

The response of Dr. Martin Luther: There has always been a church even among the papists. Among them baptism has remained and the true text of the gospel has been preserved by a divine miracle. Therefore, there were many who through that text concerning the benefits of Christ were taught to use their baptism rightly. Because they were true [168] members of the church, they were saved. Even though not in the rest of their lives, many in the last throes of death acknowledged Christ through the repeated hearing of the text of the Gospel, as, for example, my father rejected all the crazy things that were recited to him, and wanted only to believe in the Son of God. However, monks and bishops who deny Christ after baptism have been manifestly ungodly. Nevertheless some among them were also godly and were true members of the church, such as Bernhard, Bonaventure, and many other good laypersons. Thus, although not clearly, nevertheless secretly and feebly, there has been some part of the true church in the papacy.

[175] [XXV, ms. A]: Against [several theses]: Where there is the church, there is the ministry. However, the ministry requires ordinary succession. Therefore, etc.

[176] Response: It requires it, but not such as we have in the papacy. It does not require an ordinary succession bound to places. For they argue this way: Peter sits in Rome. We Roman bishops are successors of Peter. Therefore we ought to sit in Rome. This does not follow.

[Martin Luther]: Succession is bound to the gospel. If the bishop who succeeds [John Bugenhagen of] Pomerania in this church teaches the devil, I ought not obey him, because, *it states,*[1] "Flee false prophets." *According to this passage, one should see where the word is.* Not because he succeeds [*succedit*] but because he follows [*incedit*] in his footsteps. Where the word is, there is the church. *That is right.* We should not argue: Because the gospel was here in Wittenberg some years ago, therefore it is now here. [177] A bishop must be believed not because he succeeds the bishop of this place but because he teaches the gospel. *The gospel should be the* succession.

[176] [ms. B] XXV: Where the true church is, there the ministry is. Ministry requires ordinary succession, which does not exist without a political order. Therefore, the church is bound to the ordinary succession of bishops.

Response: The ministry indeed requires ordinary succession of bishops, who possess the suitable gifts for the ministry not only because of place. The adversaries teach something like this. Peter sat as the first pope in Rome. Therefore, all Roman popes in Rome following in ordinary succession possess Peter himself.

Luther [added] these things: the gospel must have succession in the church. Therefore, those who succeed true bishops in ministry but do not teach what their predecessors taught are not bishops but heretics and, as Paul says [Gal. 1:9], they are anathema, because they are not bound to the place but to the gospel. Whoever [177] teaches as their predecessors must be obeyed, if, on the contrary, they teach as heretics they must be opposed.

Excerpts from Martin Luther's Sermon on Matthew 3:13-17

Theology of the cross. "[309] But when reason comes in and wants to judge [the Trinity at Jesus' baptism], shut your eyes and senses and say, 'God has said, ["Listen to him"].' Mathematics won't work here, it is too high for that."

Jesus' baptism opens heaven once and for all. "Connect what God says to the story, so that you may learn that this event, having happened once, will never, ever cease until God finally gathers us into a visible assembly on the Last Day. [310] The text clearly says, 'John saw the heavens open,' but it continues to happen right down to today, although you and I cannot see it with our cow eyes but only with the eyes of the heart. The heavens opened themselves up and they will not again close down throughout the whole world until the Last Day when we are all inside. Note well that this story has not stopped—unlike what is said of David or others, 'He did this' [and then it was over]. Instead, the heavens have been opened from that time forward. If you see an infant baptized, or the Lord's Supper, or the absolution, or the ministry and preaching, then say, 'The heavens are open, the dove hovers, the Father's voice sounds, the Son of God stands in the water.' You dare not say, 'God shut up the heavens, we can do what we want.' If the heavens are closed, who dares baptize, preach, offer the Sacrament, absolve? This realm is called a heavenly one because Christ opened the heavens, the dove hovers, and the Father's voice sounds. So that we Christians may live more simply and honestly, thanking God that we have baptism and the word, we can think this way: 'There sits the Father, there the Son speaks, there the Holy Spirit hovers.' The Son says, 'I am with you.' For the sow and the cow, the heavens are shut, but for us, where Christ is, there the heavens are open, so that we know that Christ baptizes, preaches, absolves, and offers the Sacrament."

The Trinity's presence in the face of persecution. "For this reason, we may live holy and godly lives: because the Holy Trinity surrounds us together with all the angels, as they were there the night Christ was born. But [you say] 'God deserts us; we suffer persecution.' This happens so that your faith—that God looks after you—may be strengthened, whether you believe it or not. If you are a Christian, then heaven and earth must pass away before a hair blows in the wind. 'One who touches you, touches the apple of my eye'" [Zech. 2:8].

God's two hands. "This belongs to faith. For we do not [311] see that Christ baptizes, the Father absolves, the Holy Spirit hovers over us— not just in heaven, but he stands in the Jordan. But I say this to Christians, who ought to understand this. This is a heavenly life. According to the earthly, there is another life. But in Christianity, where the Father, Son, and Holy Spirit teach in our midst and offer the Sacrament, this is the kingdom of God, who, as Paul says, 'blesses us with all kinds of heavenly, spiritual gifts' [Eph. 2:5]. He has not showered us with trashy, earthly goods, like gold, silver, or goods, with which kings and princes are concerned and which will die with us; for we cannot take a thin dime with us. But his blessing consists in all kinds of spiritual, heavenly gifts. As Paul further says, 'He makes us sit down in the heavenly places' [Eph. 2:6], that is, on a heavenly throne, where we are judges over heavenly gifts, not worldly things, that do not belong to us—for them the world has lords and lawyers—but heavenly things. For the Christians in their individual offices are such lords as rule over death, sin, the devil and all that is a spiritual matter. They do not judge between the emperor and the pope—not like [Pope] Nicholas [actually, Gregory] and [Emperor] Henry—that's for other judges."

Pastors are lords over the devil. "I am just this sort of lord for your sakes—as you are, too. I act on your behalf. That is, when I lay my hands on the head of a poor sinner and say, 'Your sins are forgiven you,' I speak the kind of judgment that makes the devil shiver and shake. For you are declared free from the devil's power, death, law, wherever things are bothering you. In the same way, when I baptize, I declare the child free from the devil [312]. Likewise, when I offer you the Sacrament with my hand and say, 'This is the body of Christ given for you.' Likewise, when I ordain a priest and say, 'You shall be a priest.' This is proper, and the devil cannot attack it, because it has the word, the gospel. When the pope calls us heretics, he does not have a better baptism, church, Sacrament [of the Altar], or a purer, more certain anything else, or a better [Office of the] Keys (which he corrupted). Baptism, the keys, the Sacrament are right! Ach, almighty God, how you have poured over us such overwhelming riches—not only by that revelation [at the Jordan] but also that with all power [now]! Ach, how we ought to be grateful, that he gives me the power—the hand and mouth—which he himself has, because when we impose our hands, that is as valid as if God himself did it."

Common priesthood of all believers. "Moreover, suppose a preacher were not there, and my conscience were despairing. Then, if a child or a woman came to me, [I would say], 'O my dear, speak the absolution to me, lay your hands on my head.' In an emergency, that has equal authority, because that person is a member of Christ and has the power."

The public office of ministry as God's choice. "Not that the public office should be condemned—God will not stand for that. However, in an emergency, when no one else is there, the child could speak [the absolution], for just so richly has God poured out his authority and will have done whatever I do according to his command. God could have done it differently, but God didn't want to! God wanted to pour out himself and become a human being. God wanted to pour out his nature in such a way so that the human hand and mouth could establish such a great thing, that we produce children by baptizing and

forgiving them with hand and mouth, as surely as Adam and Eve produced children. What glories belong to Christians, if we only
believed it! We condemn the devil in a spiritual realm. This differs
from that human plague among people obsessed with material matters. Such things have nothing to do with us. However, in spiritual
matters, I may say, 'Begone, Satan! I absolve this one. I command you
with the power and might of God, who has commanded me.' Whatever burdens consciences, we declare free based upon the power of our
office. For God has commanded, 'What you loose . . . shall be loosed'
[Matthew 18; John 20]. Whoever has a bad conscience, go talk to a
pastor. If he is not there, go to my nearest neighbor, who should say
to me, 'Be comforted; your sins are forgiven.' This is what Paul calls,
'to sit in the heavenly places' [Eph. 2:6], that God has given us
authority over sin and death."

Pastors are powerful scum bags. "However, do not mix in temporal law
that is mortal. For here we have to do with judging spiritual matters.
'Do you not know that you will judge angels?' [1 Cor. 6:3]. That is,
the angelic beings and the devil. 'You will tread on serpents' [Ps.
91:13]. It will cause him much pain, but he must endure it because
God said to our first mother, 'The seed of the woman will crush its
head' [Gen. 3:15]. That is, Christ and his Christians are to be judge,
jury, and executioner over you. Now, this proud spirit is angered by
the fact that he has to put up with the fact that I, a poor human being,
condemn him, do you hear? 'Devil, leave my soul in peace, for Christ
has redeemed it.' But whoever could believe that anyone has such
authority, wouldn't he or she be just as happy to die as live? After all,
what are you and I compared to this glorious power? We are mortal.
There sit in the grave snakes and bugs and worms waiting to devour
us—we are no better than that. And before that time there are lice,
ticks, and fleas which would love to find a host long before we may
want to die. So what do we have in which to boast? Nevertheless, God
shall with such a tongue and hand—soon to be the food for maggots—prove to spite the devil, so that they may trample him under-
foot. No prophet, no apostle, is better than we are. Don't you think
that makes the devil angry?"

Pastors are sinners. "It's not enough that a stinking hand does such a great work and had such a heavenly authority, but it is also sinful—in fact, the heart is full of sin and evil thoughts. Yet, it shall humble that proud spirit, the devil! That one of God's own seeds, which he planted and brought forth from nature, should also be the one to restrain him. So God comes and says, 'I am going to baptize with [such a creature], bathe, preach, and he shall be my glory.' Is it not a terrible shame that we do not preach the miraculous works of God but human traditions? And we who do preach and hear—should we not also believe, rejoice, thank God, and meditate on this?"

Pastors struggle. "I am sick and tired of my flesh, this bag of worms—of the fact that I cannot and will not do these things [namely, believe, rejoice, give thanks]. O God, strike dead such cursed ungratefulness and such a sleepy, lazy listening! Send not just lice and fleas but snakes. As if this were a dead story; as if Christ were not present and the Father were not speaking! There the Father says, 'This is my Son; listen to him!' And we sleep! The Holy Spirit hovers over us! Huh? There is Christ, the Son, who says, 'I am the one who bathes you. I have made this water holy in my holy blood.' What? We sleep through such preaching and await something else. Thus, the 'scum bag' we carry around our necks hinders our believing that God pours himself out and opens heaven, that what the Father, Son, and Holy Spirit can do is ours. We still go our own way. No wonder that the pope opposes us and the Turk rules over us, given that we are so lazy and ungrateful. It's a wonder that hellfire itself doesn't rule over us!"

Grace alone; faith alone. "We should in any case learn how God proves himself to be, and likewise what he is in all his attributes and how he reveals himself: what kind of grace he shows us, how friendly and kind he is. In the next life we will see—not the form of a dove, or a voice, but face to face in his divine glory. Here we have to believe, how the three are one God, a divine life. This we believe—away with reason and its thoughts. This is what God wants: 'Look only at the Son; pay attention to him, what he does.' That is what 'well-pleased' is all about. God also is well pleased with temporal matters, such as marriage, but here he is talking about eternal blessings, so that we will no longer die, commit sin, be under the power of the devil. 'If you will listen to him, it will be well pleasing to me.' Those are powerful words, which we want to summarize in simple terms. We should know now that when we pray, baptize, preach, etc., the Holy Spirit hovers over us; the Son and the Father are by us. Wherever we believe this, sin, too, is restrained—Oh! I do not want to do evil. God hovers over me, forgives me my sins. Why shouldn't I recoil from them? But because we do not believe the word, we rush headlong into sin and shame. That is, unbelieving people who do not recognize their baptism or forget it altogether—like a sow that lies again in the muck after being washed. Soon after we have heard it, we run away, deceive others, and despise this word. But learn, please learn to honor the Christian name in your own person. Honor the clothes, in which God has dressed you for eternal life: the forgiveness of sins. Do not lie down in the muck with this garment. You would protect your silk clothes, wouldn't you? So, protect the garment of your Lord Christ. If you refuse, then know that you have lost everything, all grace and mercy done for you and your good."

Notes

1. Church Is Assembly

Portions of this chapter were first published in *Currents in Theology and Mission* 26:4 (August 1999).

1. "Holy Sonnet xviii," in Frank J. Warnke, ed., *John Donne: Poetry and Prose* (New York: Random House, 1967), 275.

2. "On the Councils and the Church," *LW* 41:148.

3. For example, Deut. 18:16; Neh. 8:2; Heb. 12:23. On *qahal* as an important symbol to the twentieth-century liturgical movement, see Louis Bouyer, *Liturgical Piety* (Notre Dame, Ind.: University of Notre Dame Press, 1955), 23–37.

4. Edward Farley, *Deep Symbols: Their Postmodern Effacement and Reclamation* (Valley Forge, Pa.: Trinity Press International, 1996).

5. See Wayne A. Meeks, *The First Urban Christians* (New Haven: Yale University Press, 1983), 108–9.

6. For a further discussion of the primitive Christian use of "assembly" as symbol, see Gordon Lathrop, *Holy People: A Liturgical Ecclesiology* (Minneapolis: Fortress Press, 1999), 29–43.

7. Pliny, *Letters* 10.96.

8. L. Michael White, *Building God's House in the Roman World* (Baltimore: Johns Hopkins University Press, 1990).

9. Justin, *1 Apology* 67.

10. Lathrop, *Holy People,* 49–71.

11. *Ut legem credendi, lex statuat supplicandi,* is the dictum taken from Prosper, *PL* 51:209. See further in Michael Church, "The Law of Begging," *Worship* 73:5 (September 1999): 442–53, and Lathrop, *Holy People,* 102–24.

12. So Luther quotes 1 Thess. 5:21 as a principle for liturgical sorting in his "Formula Missae et Communionis," *WA* 12:208.

13. Robert D. Putnam, "Bowling Alone: America's Declining Social Capital," *Journal of Democracy* 6:1 (January 1995): 65–78, and *Bowling Alone: The Collapse and Revival of American Community* (New York: Simon and Schuster, 2000).

14. Already Philip Rieff, *Fellow Teachers: Of Culture and Its Second Death* (Chicago: University of Chicago Press, 1972). Cf. Farley, *Deep Symbols,* 1, 27, 37. For what follows on culture and the "device," see also Richard Gaillardetz, "Doing Liturgy in a Technological Age," *Worship* 71 (1997): 429–51.

15. Lathrop, *Holy People,* 66.

16. Kathryn Tanner, *Theories of Culture: A New Agenda for Theology* (Guides to Theological Inquiry; Minneapolis: Fortress Press, 1997), 56–58.

17. *New York Times Magazine,* 7 December 1997.

18. Martin Luther, "The Blessed Sacrament of the Holy and True Body of Christ," 5; *LW* 35:51–52; *WA* 27:43–44.

19. Lathrop, *Holy People,* 21–48, 73–98.

20. *The Use of the Means of Grace* (Minneapolis: Evangelical Lutheran Church in America, 1997).

21. Dietrich Bonhoeffer, *Life Together and Prayerbook of the Bible,* Dietrich Bonhoeffer Works 5, trans. Daniel W. Bloesch and James H. Burtness, ed. Geffrey B. Kelly (Minneapolis: Fortress Press, 1996), 32–33.

22. Second Cor. 13:13. The apostolic greeting, accompanying the encouragement to the holy kiss and the greetings from all the other assemblies at the end of Paul's letter, is the opening greeting exchanged at the outset of many eucharistic liturgies today.

2. A Brief History of the Marks of the Church

1. Two of the most recent books on the subject do not even ask this (historical) question. Carl E. Braaten and Robert W. Jenson, eds., *Marks of the Body of Christ* (Grand Rapids: Eerdmans, 1999), and Gudrun Neebe, *Apostolische Kirche: Grundunterscheidung an Luthers Kirchenbegriff unter besonderer Berücksichtigung seiner Lehre von den* notae ecclesiae (Berlin: de Gruyter, 1997). Gudrun discusses the tract against Catharinus without realizing its true significance for the concept of the *notae ecclesiae.* See also the systematic treatment of Peter Steinacker, *Die Kennzeichen der Kirche: Eine Studie zu ihrer Einheit, Heiligkeit, Katholizität und Apostolizität* (Berlin: de Gruyter, 1982), 102–18. He begins by assuming that the list in the Nicene Creed is the normative one and, as a result, tries to force the Reformation insight into this (later!) creedal mold.

2. For example, Scott Hendrix, *Ecclesia in via: Ecclesiological Developments in the Medieval Psalms Exegesis and the Dictata super Psalterium (1513–1515) of Martin Luther* (Leiden: E. J. Brill, 1974), or Regin Prenter, *Spiritus Creator,* trans. John M. Jensen (Philadelphia: Muhlenberg, 1953). This is even true of Carl Axel Aurelius, *Verborgene Kirche: Luthers kirchenverständnis aufgrund seiner Streitschriften und Exegese 1519–1521* (Hannover: Lutherisches Verlagshaus, 1983), 43–51. He alone has examined the origins of this concept in the tracts cited below, but he does not recognize just how unique Luther's concept is, except for a reference to Werner Elert, *The Structure of Lutheranism,* trans. Walter A. Hansen (St. Louis: Concordia, 1962), 258–64.

3. Paul Althaus, *The Theology of Martin Luther* (Philadelphia: Fortress Press, 1966), 287–93; Bernhard Lohse, *Martin Luther: Eine Einführung in sein Leben und sein Werk* (Munich: Beck, 1981), 186–87 (where Lohse continues the myth that "one, holy, catholic, and apostolic" were traditionally called "marks" of the church), when in fact that association first occurred in the nineteenth century. The same is true in Lohse's more recent book, *Martin Luther's Theology: Its Historical and Systematic Development,* trans. Roy A. Harrisville (Minneapolis: Fortress Press, 1999).

4. *Oxford Dictionary of the Christian Church,* 2nd ed., F. L. Cross and E. A. Livingston, eds. (Oxford: Oxford University Press, 1974), 982–83. The third edition simply reprints the same article.

5. Johann Gerhard, *Loci theologici cum pro adstruenda veritate tum pro destruenda quorumvis contradicentium falsitate per these nervose solide et copiose explicati* (Berlin: G. Schlawitz, 1867), 5:369–601.

6. Its newness may be seen in the heading for Melanchthon's discussion of the concept in his *Loci communes theologici.* In the second edition of 1535 (*CR* 21:506) he simply stated under the topic "On the Church" *(De Ecclesia)* that "the church has external marks [*notae*], the pure word of God and the legitimate use of the sacraments." In 1543 (*CR* 21:843 and *MSA* 2/1: 528), he created a separate topic entitled "De signis monstrantibus ecclesiam, quae alii notas nominant" (concerning the signs that indicate the church, what others call marks). The "others" here may refer generally to the evangelical camp or, more directly, to Luther and to Melanchthon in the Apology and the second edition of the *Loci communes theologici.* There he also wrote (*CR* 21:507): "Quare pios etiam certam notam habere oportet, quae sit vera Ecclesia. Est autem nota certissima et praecipua, pura doctrina Evangelii" (Therefore, the godly should also have a sure mark, which is the true church. However, the most certain and chief mark is the pure teaching of the Gospel).

7. In June 1520, Luther published a response to Augustine Alveld entitled *On the Papacy in Rome against the Most Celebrated Romanist in Leipzig*. There, for the first time, he combined his argument that the church was a gathering of believers with certain external signs (German: *Zeichen*) of the church (baptism, the Lord's Supper, and the gospel). See *LW* 39:75 (*WA* 6:301).

8. See *De doctrina Christiana* 2.1.1.

9. See Zvjezdan Strika, *Johannes von Ragusa (†1443): Kirche- und Konzilsbegriff in der Auseinandersetzung mit den Hussiten und Eugen IV* (Augsburg: Wissner, 2000), 225–49. I am grateful to Gerald Christianson and Thomas Izbicki for both this reference and those to John of Torquemada.

10. See Josef Finkenzeller, "Kirche IV," *Theologische Realenzyklopädie* (Berlin: de Gruyter, 1989), 18:237: "Gegen Wyclif und Hus stellt er ausdrücklich fest, daß es sichtbare Merkmale der Kirche geben muß, daß man die Glieder der Kirche weder aufgrund der göttlichen Prädestination noch aufgrund der heiligmachenden Gnade erkennen kann." In Ulrich Kühn's article on Reformation ecclesiology that follows ("Kirche VI," 262–65), there is no mention of the origins of the marks of the church at all!

11. In *Contra epistulam Manichaei quam vocant "fundamenti,"* c. 4, n. 5 (*PL* 42:175). For an English translation, see *A Select Library of the Nicene and Post-Nicene Fathers of the Christian Church,* ed. Philip Schaff, first series, 14 vols. (reprint: Grand Rapids: Eerdmans, 1974), 4:130. For Augustine's ecclesiology, see Fritz Hofmann, *Der Kirchenbegriff des Hl. Augustinus in seinen Grundlagen und in seiner Entwicklung* (Munich: Hueber, 1933; reprint, Münster: Stenderhoff, 1978), 89–99.

12. Johannes de Ragusio [Ioannis Stojkovic], *Tractatus de Ecclesia,* ed. Franjo Sanjek (Zagreb: Varazdin, 1983), 215. I am grateful to Robert Kolb and Gerald Christianson for this reference. Augustine used neither the word *signa* nor *notae*. Ragusa's commentary reads: "In quibus verbis ad cognoscendam Caholicam ecclesiam praefatus gloriosissimus doctor ponit quinque signa et certissima indicia." A discussion of these signs then follows on pp. 216–89.

13. See especially his *Summa de Ecclesia* (Venice: Tramezino, 1561), which was also published in Rome in 1489 and in Lyons in 1496. In the early sections, Torquemada described various names for the church (bk. 1, chs. 2, pp. 3^r–4^r) and the nature of the church as containing both good and evil persons (bk. 1, chs. 3–5, pp. 4^r–7^v). He does not seem to use the notion of signs of the church, except to argue for the pope as the visible head of the church. See also Juan de Torquemada, *A Disputation on the Authority of Pope and Council,* trans. Thomas Izbicki (Oxford: Blackfriars, 1988), which includes a succinct description of his "papalist ecclesiology" by Izbicki.

14. Thomas Aquinas, *In Librum Boethii de Trinitate* 3.5.1. ra 10/4.

15. For an English translation of Ap VII.20, see *BC 2000*, 177 (*BSLK*, 239), the Latin term *notae* is translated by Justus Jonas in the German edition of the Apology as *äußerliche Zeichen* (external signs). The origins of this document at the 1530 Diet of Augsburg, its careful rhetoric, and its subsequent use as a confessional document by Lutherans make clear that it was always more than simply Melanchthon's private defense. See, for example, Timothy J. Wengert, "Philip Melanchthon's Last Word to Cardinal Lorenzo Campeggio, Papal Legate at the 1530 Diet of Augsburg," in: *Dona Melanchthoniana: Festgabe für Heinz Scheible zum 70. Geburtstag,* ed. Johanna Loehr (Stuttgart-Bad Cannstatt: Frommann-Holzboog, 2001), 457–83.

16. Hence, in the *Loci communes theologici* of 1543 he used the phrase *signa monstralia ecclesiam,* signs pointing out the church. His admission that the word *nota* was new (*"quae alii notas nominant*; "what others call *notae*") probably represented a muted response to Roman criticisms of the use of this term in the Apology. There is no such comment in either the second edition of 1535 or in the German translation (by Melanchthon) of 1555.

17. The confusion between the evangelical marks of the church and the "one, holy, catholic, and apostolic," appears in recent work on Melanchthon's thought and especially in commentaries on the Augsburg Confession. For a summary of the discussion, see Gunther Wenz, *Theologie der Bekenntnisschriften der evangelisch-lutherischen Kirche: Eine historische und systematische Einführung in das Konkordienbuch,* 2 vols. (Berlin: de Gruyter, 1996, 1998), 2:259–60, 267–68, 300–315. Without realizing it, Wenz passes on the modern systematic confusion between the phrases in the Nicene Creed and the use of the term during the Reformation.

18. *LW* 34:287; *WA* 50:659.

19. Ambrogio Catarino Politi.

20. "Answer to the Hyperchristian, Hyperspiritual, and Hyperlearned Book by Goat Emser in Leipzig—Including Some Thoughts regarding His Companion, the Fool Murner," *LW* 39:137–224; *WA* 7:621–88.

21. In the earlier tract against Alveld, Luther used the term in passing. See below.

22. See Scott Hendrix, *Luther and the Papacy: Stages in a Reformation Conflict* (Philadelphia: Fortress Press, 1981), 46–52.

23. *WA* 7:719, 26–28.

24. In the Donatist heresy of the fourth and fifth centuries in North Africa, the church divided over whether bishops ordained by bishops suspected of handing over the sacred books during persecution were true bishops.

Donatists, like some groups among the Puritans, argued that only a pure clergy could bear the gospel.

25. *WA* 7:719, 34–720, 4.

26. This is not, however, the same as arguing that therefore a particular church cannot decide to use a particular order and enforce it on its members. The question must always be whether the imposition of a particular order, say, episcopal, hinders or prevents the proclamation of the gospel. If it does not, then those who object to such changes more than likely are also arguing that to be church a particular order must be preserved (and thus are themselves "anti-church").

27. *WA* 7:720, 4–12.

28. See Timothy J. Wengert, "Adiaphora," *Oxford Encyclopedia of the Reformation*, 4 vols. (New York: Oxford University Press, 1996), 1:4–7.

29. See especially Luther's Invocavit sermons of 1522 in *LW* 51:67–100; *WA* 10³:1–64.

30. See not only *LW* 40:263–320 (*WA* 26:195–240) but also the correspondence by Melanchthon (one of the official Saxon visitors) involving the nuns at Cronschwitz (*MBW* 567 [*T3*:111, 103–13, 172] and *MBW* 585 [*T3*:152–54]).

31. *WA* 7:720, 32–38 (emphasis added).

32. *WA* 7:720, 38–721, 9. Throughout the tract, Luther made fun of the fact that Catharinus referred to himself and Prierias as distinguished teachers.

33. *WA* 7:721, 9–14.

34. Later, in the Large Catechism and elsewhere, Luther would incorporate the sacraments themselves into this activity of the gospel by defining them (in Augustinian fashion) as visible words.

35. *WA* 7:721, 15–20.

36. Eric Gritsch, *Martin—God's Court Jester: Luther in Retrospect* (Philadelphia: Fortress Press, 1983), 98, quoting *WA* 10¹,²:48, 5. It is also translated in *Sermons of Martin Luther,* ed. John Lenker, 8 vols. (reprint; Grand Rapids: Baker, 1989), 1:44.

37. See Fred W. Meuser, *Luther the Preacher* (Minneapolis: Augsburg, 1983), 24–25.

38. *WA* 39¹: 334–58, cited in James A. Nestingen, "Preaching Repentance," *Lutheran Quarterly,* n.s., 3 (1989): 253.

39. *WA* 7:721, 29–34.

40. *WA* 7:722, 3–4, 13–17.

41. *LW* 39:218; *WA* 7:683.

42. Among others, Paul Althaus implies this in *The Theology of Martin Luther,* 293, where he distinguishes between Luther's polemics and Luther's calmer positive assessment of the visible church.

3. The Marks of the Church in the Liturgy

Portions of this chapter were first published in *Grundtvig Studier* 2000 and in *Worship* 75:1 (January 2001).

1. *LW* 41:148. The essay is "Von den Conziliis und Kirchen," in *WA* 50:509–653. The English translation of this essay is "On the Councils and the Church," in *LW* 41:9–178.

2. *LW* 41:151; cf. 148–66.

3. Ibid., 150.

4. Ibid., 153.

5. Ibid., 156, 164.

6. Ibid.,165.

7. *CA* VII:1–4, trans. of the German text; *BC 2000,* 42.

8. *The Use of the Means of Grace: A Statement on the Practice of Word and Sacrament* (Minneapolis: Augsburg Fortress, 1997).

9. Minneapolis: Augsburg, and Philadelphia: Board of Publication, 1978.

10. For N. F. S. Grundtvig, his writings, his extensive influence on the Danish church, and his importance for contemporary liturgical renewal, see especially A. M. Allchin, *N. F. S. Grundtvig: An Introduction to His Life and Work* (Aarhus: Aarhus University Press, 1997).

11. Johannes Knudsen, ed., *N. F. S. Grundtvig: Selected Writings* (Philadelphia: Fortress Press, 1976), 54–63.

12. *Den christelige Børnelærdom,* quoted as "Basic Christian Teachings" in Knudsen, 81.

13. Ibid., 80.

14. "Kun ved badet og ved bordet, hører vi Guds ord til os."

15. "For disse bestemte ord i dåbs- og nadverritualerne udtrykker for Grundtvig det kristne budskab i al dets fylde. Disse bestemte ord bliver den hermeneutiske nøgle både for hans prædiken og for hans salmer." Christian Thodberg, "Grundtvig og den danske gudstjenestetradition i internationalt perspektiv" (unpublished paper, 1997), 19.

16. Kenneth W. Stevenson, "Grundtvig's Hymns from an Anglican Point of View," A. A. Allchin, et al., eds., *Heritage and Prophecy: Grundtvig and the English-Speaking World* (Norwich. Canterbury Press, 1994), 167.

17. Christian Thodberg, "Grundtvig," 20: "en folkelig sakramental vækkelse."

18. Knudsen, *Grundtvig,* 59, emphasis added.

19. For one account, see Enok Mortensen, *Stories from Our Church* (Des Moines: Committee on Publications of the Danish Evangelical Lutheran Church of America, 1952), 94–109.

20. The origin of the bell is unknown, but Edwin Pedersen, a parish historian in Luck, Wisconsin, believes that in the nineteenth century it first hung in the Danish church in Hutchinson, Minnesota, and came to the steeple of the second West Denmark church building in 1938.

21. Cf. Jens Holger Schjørring, "Grundtvig, the Oxford Movement and Rationalist Theology," *Heritage and Prophecy,* 231.

22. Christian Thodberg, "The Importance of Baptism in Grundtvig's View of Christianity," in Allchin, *Heritage and Prophecy,* 140–42.

23. For an example of the prayer standing next to the bath and the table as places of the presence of God in the assembly, as full of the voice of the Lord, see Grundtvig's hymn, "Herrens røst var over vandet," *Den Danske Salmebog* (Copenhagen: Det kgl. Vajsenhus' Forlag, 1967), 346.

24. Christian Thodberg, on "The Importance of Baptism" in "Grundtvig," 134.

25. Martin Luther, "A Brief Instruction on What to Look for and Expect in the Gospels," *LW* 35:121.

26. This insight belongs especially to Cantor Mark Mummert of the Lutheran Theological Seminary at Philadelphia.

27. *Skal den Lutherske Reformation virkelig fortsættes?* (Copenhagen: Schauberg, 1863), 115–16, quoted in Allchin, *Heritage and Prophecy,* 118; translation altered. About the learned, Grundtvig says: "Og de Skrift-Kløge vaage over Bogen med Nat-Lampen tændet ved Alter-Lyset, og vaage over at Kirken har aabne Dørre, til Adgang saavelsom til Indgang."

4. The Marks of the Church in *The Book of Concord*

1. See Charles Arand, *Testing the Boundaries: Windows to Lutheran Identity* (St. Louis: Concordia, 1995).

2. See Robert Kolb, *Confessing the Faith: Reformers Define the Church, 1530–1580* (St. Louis: Concordia, 1991), 46–49. This explains why Luther, preaching at the funeral of Elector John of Saxony in 1532, could comfort his hearers by announcing that their prince, by virtue of his confessing, had died in 1530 at Augsburg. See *LW* 51:231–55; *WA* 36:237–70.

3. For example, Leif Grane, *The Augsburg Confession: A Commentary* (Minneapolis: Augsburg, 1987), does not discuss CA XXII–XXVIII. Wilhelm Maurer, *Historical Commentary on the Augsburg Confession*, trans. H. George Anderson (Philadelphia: Fortress Press, 1986), writes as though CA XXVIII was somehow the key to the entire document. Many commentators either divide it up into theological loci or ignore the structure altogether. For one author who tries to overcome this problem, see Gunther Wenz, *Theologie der Bekenntnisschriften der evangelisch-lutherischen Kirche: Eine historische und systematische Einführung in das Konkordienbuch*, 2 vols. (Berlin: de Gruyter, 1996, 1998), especially, for example, his discussion of works and faith in 2:176–97.

4. See Timothy J. Wengert, "Philip Melanchthon's Last Word to Cardinal Lorenzo Campeggio, Papal Legate at the 1530 Diet of Augsburg," in: *Dona Melanchthoniana: Festgabe für Heinz Scheible zum 70. Geburtstag,* ed. Johanna Loehr (Stuttgart: Fromman-Holzboog, 2001), 457–83.

5. This approach was popularized by Wilhelm Maurer.

6. Although CA XVII also reflects the language of the Second Article and Christ's return, the topic was typically covered in relation to the third article of the creed and the resurrection of the dead.

7. See Timothy J. Wengert, *Human Freedom, Christian Righteousness: Philip Melanchthon's Exegetical Dispute with Erasmus of Rotterdam* (New York: Oxford University Press, 1998).

8. Eck published his charges in Augsburg in April 1530 in his *404 Articles*. See *Sources and Contexts of the Book of Concord,* ed. Robert Kolb and James A. Nestingen (Minneapolis: Fortress Press, 2001), 31–82.

9. *BC 2000,* 38 and 40. The Latin text reads (pp. 39 and 41): "Likewise, they teach that human beings cannot be justified before God by their own powers, merits, or works. But they are justified as a gift on account of Christ through faith when they believe that they are received into grace and that their sins are forgiven on account of Christ, who by his death made satisfaction for our sins. God reckons this faith as righteousness (Romans 3 and 4). So that we may obtain this faith, the ministry of teaching the gospel and administering the sacraments was instituted. For through the Word and the sacraments as through instruments the Holy Spirit is given, who effects faith where and when it pleases God in those who hear the gospel, that is to say, in those who hear that God, not on account of our own merits, but on account of Christ, justifies those who believe that they are received into grace on account of Christ. Galatians 3[:14b]: 'So that we might receive the promise of the Spirit through faith.' They condemn the Anabaptists and

others who think that the Holy Spirit comes to human beings without the external Word through their own preparations and works."

10. A footnote in the earlier English edition of *The Book of Concord,* ed. Theodore Tappert (Philadelphia: Fortress Press, 1959), 31, at this point mistranslated a line from the footnotes of the critical edition with the word "clerical" instead of "clericalistic." This allowed people to argue that the "office of preaching" here was not referring to the public office of ministry.

11. See Heiko A. Oberman, *The Harvest of Medieval Theology: Gabriel Biel and Late Medieval Nominalism* (Grand Rapids: Eerdmans, 1967). It is no accident that in the response to Luther's *On the Bondage of the Will,* the two-volume *Hyperaspistes,* Erasmus used Gabriel Biel to refute Luther.

12. Gerhard O. Forde, "The Ordained Ministry," in: *Called and Ordained,* ed. Marc Kolden and Todd Nichol (Minneapolis: Fortress Press, 1990), 117–36.

13. *BC 2000,* 42. The Latin (p. 43) reads: "Likewise, they teach that one holy church will remain forever. The church is the assembly of saints in which the gospel is taught purely and the sacraments are administered rightly. And it is enough for the true unity of the church to agree concerning the teaching of the gospel and the administration of the sacraments. It is not necessary that human traditions, rites, or ceremonies instituted by human beings be alike everywhere. As Paul says [Ephesians 4:5,6]: 'One faith, one baptism, one God and Father of all. . . .' Although the church is, properly speaking, the assembly of saints and those who truly believe, nevertheless, because in this life many hypocrites and evil people are mixed in with them, a person may use the sacraments even when they are administered by evil people. This accords with the saying of Christ [Matthew 23:2]: 'The scribes and the Pharisees sit on Moses' seat. . . .' Both the sacraments and the Word are efficacious because of the ordinance and command of Christ, even when offered by evil people. They condemn the Donatists and others like them who have denied the ministry of evil people may be used in the church and who have thought that the ministry of evil people is useless and ineffective."

14. *BC 2000,* 48. The Latin (p. 49) reads: "Concerning church rites they teach that those rites should be observed that can be observed without sin and that contribute to peace and good order in the church, for example, certain holy days, festivals, and the like. However, people are reminded not to burden consciences, as if such worship were necessary for salvation. They are also reminded that human traditions that are instituted to win God's favor,

merit grace, and make satisfaction for sins are opposed to the gospel and the teaching of faith. That is why vows and traditions concerning foods and days, etc., instituted to merit grace and make satisfaction for sins, are useless and contrary to the gospel."

15. An early example was the exchange between Gerhard O. Forde and Michael Root at the conference of ELCA theologians held in Techny, Illinois, in 1990.

16. CA XX.8–9, 23, 27 (German), in *BC 2000*, 54, 56.

17. For a handy summary of the issues, see Wenz, *Theologie der Bekenntnisschriften*, 2:370–412.

18. See Timothy J. Wengert, "Certificate of Ordination (1545) for George von Anhalt, Coadjutor Bishop of Merseburg," *Lutheran Quarterly*, n.s., 16 (2002): 229–33.

19. CA XXVIII.5, 8, 10 (German), in *BC 2000*, 92.

20. CA XXVIII.21 (German), in *BC 2000*, 94.

21. Ap VII/VIII.20, in *BC 2000*, 177.

22. Ap VII/VIII.31, in *BC 2000*, 179.

23. Tr 60, in *BC 2000*, 340.

24. Tr 67, in *BC 2000*, 340–41.

25. SC, Creed, 6, in *BC 2000*, 355.

26. *WA* 11:54, 4–9.

27. LC, Creed, 42, in *BC 2000*, 436.

28. Ibid.

29. LC, Creed, 43, in *BC 2000*, 436.

30. LC, Creed, 45, in *BC 2000*, 436.

31. Jay Beech, "The Church Song," *Worship and Praise* (Minneapolis: Augsburg Fortress, 1999), no. 135.

32. LC, Creed, 51–53, in *BC 2000*, 437–38.

33. SA III.12.1, in *BC 2000*, 324.

34. SA III.12.2, in *BC 2000*, 324.

35. SA III.12.2, in *BC 2000*, 324–25.

36. SA III.12.3, in *BC 2000*, 325.

37. In this regard, Luther's pointed attack on "enthusiasm," worship of the god within (with no respect for the external word of the gospel) is particularly important. See SA III.8.3–13, in *BC 2000*, 322–23.

38. SD XII.14, in *BC 2000*, 657.

39. SD XII.15, in *BC 2000*, 657.

40. SD XII.27, in *BC 2000*, 658.

41. Cf. Ep X, in *BC 2000, 515.*
42. Ep X.3, in *BC 2000, 515.*
43. Ep X.4, in *BC 2000, 515.*
44. Ep X.5, in *BC 2000, 515.*
45. Ep X.7, in *BC 2000, 516.*
46. Ibid.

5. The Marks of the Church in the Later Luther

1. Gudrun Neebe, *Apostolische Kirche: Grundunterscheidungen an Luthers Kirchenbegriff unter besonderer Berücksichtigung seiner Lehre von den* notae ecclesiae (Berlin: de Gruyter, 1997), also examines many of these documents, but from a strictly systematic perspective. For discussion of Luther's *On the Councils and the Churches* of 1539 and the so-called Visitation Articles of 1527/28, see chapters 3 and 6 by Gordon Lathrop in this volume.

2. John Eck, *Enchiridion of Commonplaces against Luther and Other Enemies of the Church,* trans. Ford Lewis Battles (Grand Rapids: Baker, 1979), 16. Eck's use of the term "mathematical," a sixteenth-century equivalent for "speculative" or "abstract," calls to mind the importance of the distinction in Thomas Aquinas between abstract concepts that need mathematics and sensible things that have *notae.*

3. *LW* 13:90; *WA* 403:506-7.

4. *WA* 46:285.

5. Luther constructed another similar list in *Against Hanswurst* (1541), *LW* 41:194–98; *WA* 51:479–85.

6. *LW* 40:41; *WA* 12:194. Melanchthon used this distinction in CA VII.

7. *LW* 40:44; *WA* 12:196.

8. *LW* 16:32; *WA* 31^2:22f.

9. *LW* 38:196; *WA* 38:237.

10. The same phrase Philip Melanchthon used in the *Loci communes* of 1543.

11. *WA* 41:240.

12. *LW* 13:89; *WA* 40^3:506.

13. LC, Lord's Prayer, 7, in *BC 2000,* 441.

14. *LW* 54:476; *WA TR* 5:317f. (no. 5677).

15. Ap XIII.11, in *BC 2000,* 220.

16. *LW* 38:197; *WA* 38:238. By "little bishop" Luther meant that Augustine was a bishop in a small town.

17. *LW* 5:244; *WA* 43:597.

18. *LW* 5:248; *WA* 43:600.

19. The classical definition of this topic in Luther's thought is still Walter von Loewenich, *Luther's Theology of the Cross*, trans. Herbert J. A. Bouman (Minneapolis: Augsburg, 1976). See also Gerhard O. Forde, *On Being a Theologian of the Cross* (Grand Rapids: Eerdmans, 1997).

20. *LW* 5:248; *WA* 43:600.

21. *LW* 5:249, altered; *WA* 43:600.

22. *LW* 40:42; *WA* 12:195.

23. *WA* 59:175.

24. *LW* 1:253; *WA* 42:187.

25. *LW* 2:197; *WA* 42:401.

26. Parker Palmer, in a lecture delivered at the Lutheran Theological Seminary at Philadelphia in 1991.

27. *WA* 34^1:460, 7.

28. *WA* 40^3:54, 3.

29. *LW* 3:37; *WA* 42:575.

30. *LW* 53:304–5; *WA* 35:467–68. See also *The Lutheran Book of Worship* (Minneapolis: Augsburg, and Philadelphia: Board of Publication, 1978), no. 230.

31. *WA* 39^1:166, 10–11.

32. *WA* 39^1:166, 14–17.

33. *LW* 40:42; *WA* 12:194–95.

34. *LW* 13:89; *WA* 40^3:505.

35. *WA* 41:700.

36. *LW* 6:149; *WA* 44:111.

37. *LW* 26:24–25; *WA* 40:69–70.

38. *LW* 5:245; *WA* 53:597.

39. *WA* 41:241.

40. *WA* 41:242. Here, Luther seemed to be appealing to the practice of confirming a baptism done by a midwife. Rather than view that baptism as incomplete and the worship service as validating the imperfect work of a woman, Luther saw the opposite. The church's confirmation proved that God was at work in the woman baptizing all along, because the marks Christ gives to the church are sure.

41. *LW* 40:41; *WA* 12:194. This had concrete results when, in fact, Luther did this with the installation of Georg von Anhalt as coadjutor of the diocese of Merseburg. See Timothy J. Wengert, "Certificate of Ordination (1545) for George von Anhalt, Coadjutor Bishop of Merseburg," *Lutheran Quarterly*, n.s., 16 (2002): 229–33. This certificate was drafted by Melanchthon and signed by Luther.

42. *LW* 38:196; *WA* 38:237. The word *Pfarrherr* (pastor) did not designate every ordained person but only the chief pastor in a particular town or city. Thus, Johannes Bugenhagen was the *Pfarrherr* in Wittenberg.

43. *LW* 4:348; *WA* 43:387.

44. *LW* 4:348–49; *WA* 43:387.

45. *LW* 4:406–7; *WA* 43:428.

46. *LW* 4:407; *WA* 43:428.

47. *WA* 39²:145–84. For a translation of the theses, see Appendix 1. His last name started with Mac, hence the nickname.

48. *WA* 392:146–48.

49. This, of course, happens more easily if one understands the church to be an institution and not an event.

50. Timothy J. Wengert, "Martin Luther's Movement toward an Apostolic Self-Awareness as Reflected in His Early Letters," *Luther-Jahrbuch* 61 (1994): 71–92.

51. For example, some argue that preventing other people than bishops to ordain is a *status confessionis*. This would only be true if the bishop forbade the preaching of the gospel, which none of the opponents to such a practice have ever even attempted to demonstrate.

52. *WA* 39²:161.

53. *WA* 39²:161.

54. *WA* 39²:167–68. Italicized portions are in German in the original.

55. *WA* 39²:176–77. Italicized portions are in German in the original.

56. *WA* 39²:176–77.

57. *WA* 39²:178. See also Luther's sermon on this text from 1538.

58. *WA* 39²:179.

59. *WA* 39²:181.

60. *WA* 39²:181–82.

61. *WA* 49:308–17.

62. Excerpts from this sermon are translated in Appendix 2, with headings that correspond (mutatis mutandis) to what follows.

63. *WA* 49:309. Cf. p. 153.

64. *WA* 49:309–10. Cf. p. 153–54.

65. *WA* 49:310. Cf. p. 154.

66. *WA* 49:311. Cf. p. 154.

67. *WA* 49:311–12. Cf. p. 155.

68. *WA* 49:312. Cf. p. 155–56

69. In the seventeenth and eighteenth centuries, certain pietists were interested in creating "the young Luther," who had not yet been affected by

Philip Melanchthon's orthodoxy. Thus, early documents emphasizing the congregation's role in selecting pastors became an excuse to blame the old Luther for abandoning this pious, egalitarian ordering of ministry.

70. This is what some church presidents imagine when they get mad at the pastors or when there is a vacancy. A healthier approach to Luther's ecclesiology is demonstrated by the Rev. Roy Riley, the ELCA bishop of New Jersey and the author's own bishop. When he meets with a congregation in a vacancy, he reminds the congregation that it has two pastors, one of whom has left. He is the other pastor, there to serve the congregation by making sure that worship continues and that a new pastor is found.

71. *WA* 49:313. Cf. p. 156.

72. *WA* 49:313–14. Cf. p. 157.

73. *WA* 49:314. Cf. p. 157.

74. *WA* 49:314–15. Cf. p. 157–58.

6. The Marks of the Church as a Theme for the Visitation of Parishes

Portions of this chapter were first published in *Worship* 72:6 (November 1998).

1. Let the name stand for regional ministers, servants of a regional church, whatever the title of that office: bishop, superintendent, conference minister, etc.

2. CA XXVIII:8; *BC 2000,* 92.

3. *LW* 40:269–320.

4. *The Use of the Means of Grace: A Statement on the Practice of Word and Sacrament* (Minneapolis: Augsburg Fortress, 1997).

5. Excerpts from Part I, "Biblical and Theological Foundations," of "Towards Koinonia in Worship: Report of the Consultation" held in Ditchingham, England, August 1994, and published in Thomas F. Best and Dagmar Heller, *So We Believe, So We Pray: Towards Koinonia in Worship,* Faith and Order Paper 171 (Geneva: World Council of Churches, 1995), 5–8.

6. Walt Kallestad, *Entertainment Evangelism* (Nashville: Abingdon, 1996), 42, 78–79, 123–26; G. A. Pritchard, *Willow Creek Seeker Services* (Grand Rapids: Baker, 1996), 49–55.

7. Kallestad, *Entertainment Evangelism,* 23, 60–61; Lynne and Bill Hybels, *Rediscovering Church* (Grand Rapids: Zondervan, 1995), 23–42.

8. Paul K. Conkin, *Cane Ridge: America's Pentecost* (Madison: University of Wisconsin Press, 1990), 18, 105.

9. R. Laurence Moore, *Selling God* (New York: Oxford University Press, 1994), 47.

10. Conkin, *Cane Ridge,* 164.

11. See especially, Harold Bloom, *The American Religion* (New York: Simon and Schuster, 1992), 59–75.

12. James F. White, *Protestant Worship: Traditions in Transition* (Louisville: Westminster John Knox, 1989), 171–91.

13. Conkin, *Cane Ridge,* 168.

14. Ibid.

15. Eberhard Weismann, "Der Predigtgottesdienst und die verwandten Formen," in *Leiturgia* 3 (Kassel: Stauda, 1956): 19ff.

16. Charles Grandison Finney, *Lectures on Revivals of Religion,* ed. William G. McLoughlin (Cambridge: Harvard University Press, 1960), 250.

17. Finney, *Lectures,* 251.

18. Cf. White, *Protestant Worship,* 177.

19. Ibid.

20. I thank my colleague Thomas H. Schattauer for this point.

21. On the Willow Creek editing of Calvinism, see Pritchard, *Willow Creek,* 46–47.

22. Ibid., 183; cf. 179ff.

23. Hybels, *Rediscovering Church,* 169–81; Pritchard, *Willow Creek,* 23–26.

24. Kallestad, *Entertainment Evangelism,* 107–18.

25. David S. Luecke, *The Other Story of Lutherans at Worship* (Tempe, Ariz.: Fellowship Ministries, 1995), 6–22.

26. Thus, Robert Schuller.

27. Luecke, *Other Story,* 89–90.

28. Frank C. Senn, "'Worship Alive': An Analysis and Critique of 'Alternative Worship Services,'" *Worship* 69:3 (May 1995): 203.

29. Randolph Sly, "Convergence Worship," in Robert E. Webber, ed., *The Complete Library of Christian Worship* 3 (Nashville: Star Song, 1993), 196–99.

30. See Charles Yrigoyen and George Bricker, eds., *Catholic and Reformed: Selected Theological Writings of John Williamson Nevin* (Pittsburgh: Pickwick, 1978).

31. It is interesting to note that active insiders at Willow Creek sometimes come to doubt whether other insiders have been appropriately saved or made the correct, saving decision. One staff member is quoted as saying, "I don't think Bill Hybels really understands that there are as many unsaved

people—who think they're saved—around here as there are" (Pritchard, *Willow Creek,* 278).

32. *WA* 51:193; translation altered from *LW* 51:390–91.

8. The Historian Reads the Liturgist

1. Timothy J. Wengert, "Melanchthon and Luther / Luther and Melanchthon," *Luther-Jahrbuch* 66 (1999): 55–88.

2. It is no small irony that the church where I am worshiping during this sabbatical, Christ the King Lutheran Church in Houston, has a bell tower with three bells still rung three times each day, donated by a Norwegian American builder who knew the power of such instruments to draw "every seeking soul."

3. In the words of Luther's explanation to the introduction to the Lord's Prayer in the Small Catechism.

4. See Timothy J. Wengert, *Law and Gospel: Philip Melanchthon's Debate with John Agricola of Eisleben over* Poenitentia (Grand Rapids: Baker, 1997), 94–145.

5. SC, Creed, 6, in *BC 2000,* 355–56.

Appendix 1:
The Promotion Disputation of Johann Macchabäus of Scotland

The disputation was held on 3 February 1542, Martin Luther presiding (*WA* 39²: 145–84). This text was translated by Timothy J. Wengert. The numbers in brackets refer to the pages in the *WA.*

1. The italicized portions are in German.

Appendix 2:
Excerpts from Martin Luther's Sermon on Matthew 3:13-17

Preached on the First Sunday after the Epiphany (the Baptism of Jesus), 13 January 1544. *WA* 49:308–17. The text was translated by Timothy J. Wengert. The numbers in brackets refer to pages in the *WA.* The italicized introductions refer to sections in chapter 5.

Index

Trinity, 107–8

Use of the Means of Grace, 14, 42,
  160, 115
Uvdal church, 135

Vannorsdall, John, 137
Vincent of Lérins, 9
Visitation articles, 26, 115, 170
Visitation of parishes, 114–16,
  121, 130–31

Weismann, Eberhard, 174
Wenz, Gunther, 163, 167, 169

West Denmark Lutheran Church,
  46, 166
White, James F., 123
White, L. Michael, 6–7, 159
Word, 29–31, 33, 47–48, 58–60,
  63–64, 72–73, 84–85, 97,
  105–6, 139
World Council of Churches, 116
Wycliffe, John, 20

Zwingli, Ulrich, 66